MY
P-R-A-Y-E-R
JOURNAL

A 90-DAY JOURNEY TO A MORE
FULFILLED PRAYER LIFE

RALPH SPILLER

WestBow
PRESS
A DIVISION OF THOMAS NELSON

Unless otherwise indicated, Scripture quotations are from the King James Version.

Quotations of E. M. Bounds from A 12-Month Guide to BETTER PRAYER used by permission from Barbour Publishing, P. O. Box 719, Uhrichsville, Ohio, 44683

WestBow Press books may be ordered through booksellers or by contacting:

WestBow Press
A Division of Thomas Nelson
1663 Liberty Drive
Bloomington, IN 47403
www.westbowpress.com
1-(866) 928-1240

ISBN: 978-1-4497-7141-6 (sc)
ISBN: 978-1-4497-7140-9 (e)

Library of Congress Control Number: 2012920416

Printed in the United States of America

WestBow Press rev. date: 11/02/2012

To the glory of God, and my LORD and Savior, Jesus Christ

To my loving wife, Barbara.

To the publishing staff at WestBow Press, who so patiently guided the production of this prayer journal.

To the friends who have supported the development of this prayer journal through their prayers and encouragement.

PREFACE

Welcome to a journey with the God of your creation in the exploration of His will for your life and the depth, height, and breadth of His grace through prayer. Prayer is a discipline of the walk with God in communion with Him that is the weakest of all of the disciplines in the Christian walk. Charles Spurgeon and E. M. Bounds were renowned preachers, teachers, and authors of the late nineteenth and early twentieth centuries. They were great men of prayer who, even a century and more ago, spoke of the weakness of the prayer life of the church, and the resulting powerlessness of the church of today in contrast to that of the apostles and the church of the first century. I have great admiration for these writers along with many of the writers of today.

This journal is not intended to become a ritual to be performed but rather as an instrument used to develop the discipline of prayer, of communion with our LORD, that in developing this conversational relationship with Him, He will perform what we ask according to His will, to His glory, and to the benefit of others and self. Prayer is intended to reveal the glory of God with the benefit falling on others and self as the revelation of God. Prayer is not to be the means to the end of causing God to bend to our wills as we make our petitions to Him.

Prayer apart from a study of the Word of God is but words uttered into the air that result in a false sense of well-being with the God to whom we have been *'praying.'* True prayer is communion with God in search of His will, in finding understanding of His will, in more fully applying the truth of His will in our daily walk, and in expression of gratitude as He grants to you of His bountiful grace revealing the Persons of the Trinity.

Prayer is not seeking the service *of* God (as is often the case), but service *to* God by a grateful and obedient people.

How does one approach the throne of God, as we are invited and encouraged to do (Hebrews 4:16)? A study of the Temple of Israel will give insight to the requirements as established by God; however, as such a study is left to other works, it is not therefore the purpose of this journal of your journey with God. We are to be cleansed, made pure in His sight, for He cannot look upon sin. Sin separates the pray-er from fellowship with God. We who are in Christ are cleansed *before* we enter His presence so that we may enter communion with Him (Hebrews 10:19). In His presence, we search—with Him—to discover His will and His purpose for us. Many come to God simply to tell Him what they want Him to do for them. (By the way, "telling" is not the same as "asking," which we are invited and encouraged to do.) Before Him, we must remember who we are so that we might know who He is. It is in knowing Him that we can ask, seek, and knock as we are invited to do (Matthew 7:7-8).

The concept for this book is based on the acronym—

P-R-A-Y-E-R

—to present a method to remember the elements of prayer. These elements appear as follows on each page:

Praise and Thanksgiving
Repentance through Confession
Ask (for needs of others and self)
Yield to the Father
Examine and
Reflect

The last two letters, and the words associated, may cause some people to question the ideas expressed here. However, our prayer life needs to be examined by asking questions of ourselves, such as, "Have I exhibited humility in my praying?" "Have I allowed Satan to creep in, attacking through my weaknesses?" "Am I seeking the will of God, or the will of the flesh? or "Am I truly seeking the will of God or to impress God with my will?" This examination and reflection will help us to grow in self-awareness and God-awareness to reflect on our motivation regarding our requests of God. James writes, "Ye ask, and receive not, because ye ask amiss (from self-centered motivation), that ye may consume it upon your lusts" (James 4:3). To derive the greatest enrichment in this journey, one will need to study and meditate upon the Biblical references for each section each day that you may grasp the context of the passage and record insight gained.

Also of note, you will find the abundance of space to record other notes as the result of meditation on Scripture. Martin Luther said, "To pray well is to have studied well." Daily devotional readings are strongly encouraged when communing with God. Then record what God says in response to your reading and your speaking to Him.

It is my prayer that you will find a deeper, more enriched prayer life as you venture on this journey that will then lead you to live as Christ living in and through you; that you will then experience the blessing of God in ways you may never have imagined; and that you will not set this book aside as you *finish* this journey but will repeat this journey again and again.

EXAMPLE PAGES

This page and the next are examples to show the suggested use of the journal.

Date_____

"And this is the confidence that we have in Him, that, if we ask anything according to His will, He heareth us: And if we know that He hear us, whatsoever we ask, we know that we have the petitions that we desired if Him."   I John 5:14-15

Praise and Thanksgiving
"O Come, let us sing unto the LORD: let us make a joyful noise to the rock of our salvation . . . O come, let us worship and bow down: let us kneel before the LORD our Maker."   Psalm 95:1, 6

   Insert words of praise - the character of God, i.e. "God, our Creator, God of grace and mercy" (search other 'names of God' in Scripture); words of thanks-giving, i.e. "Thank you for hearing my prayer, for the peace and comfort of Your presence."

_____

_____

Repent through Confession
'Therefore say thou unto them, Thus saith the LORD of hosts; Turn ye unto Me, saith the LORD of hosts, and I will turn unto you, saith the LORD of hosts."   Zechariah 1:3

"Draw nigh to God, and He will draw nigh unto you. Cleanse your hands, ye sinners; and purify your hearts, ye double minded."   James 4:8

Words of confession acknowledging before Him ways in which, through attitude and action, you have gone against His will. Seek his guidance and power to overcome your tendency to go against His will.

_____

_____

<u>A</u>sk

"Ask, and it shall be given you; seek, and you shall find; knock, and it shall be opened unto you: for everyone that asketh receiveth; and he that seeketh findeth; and to him that knocketh it shall be opened."

Matthew 7:7-8

Salvation

"For by grace are you saved through faith; . . . it is the gift of God"

Ephesians 2:8

Name	Date Entered	Date Answered

Enter names of persons laid upon your heart regarding their relationship with God, and the date; others will be added in weeks following.

<u>Y</u>ield to the Father (Prayer of surrender to the will of the Father)

"Nevertheless not what I will, but what thou wilt."   Mark 14:36b

(A prayer of surrender)

<u>E</u>xamine and <u>R</u>eflect

"Examine yourselves, whether ye be in faith; prove your own selves."

2 Corinthians 13:5

(Meditate regarding the *true condition* of praying)

(Is my prayer seeking God's will and guidance to achieve His will?)

(What has God revealed to me in my communion and communication with Him?)

Notes

The Siamese Twins of Prayer

Faith is always praying.
Prayer is always believing.
Faith must have a tongue by which it can speak.
Prayer is the tongue of faith.
Faith must receive.
Prayer is the hand of faith stretched out to receive.

Prayer must rise and soar.
Faith must give prayer the wings to fly and soar.
Prayer must have an audience with God.
Faith opens the door, and access and audience are given.
Prayer asks.
Faith lays its hand on the thing asked for.

Bounds, E. M., "Prayer - Its Possibilities," *A 12-Month Guide to Better Prayer.* Barbour Publishing, Inc., Uhrichsville, OH 44683, www.barbourbooks.com.

Date_____

"He hears and answers every prayer, where the *true conditions* of praying are met." (*italics* inserted for emphasis)

E. M. Bounds, "The Possibilities of Prayer"

"And this is the confidence that we have in Him, that, if we ask anything according to His will, He heareth us: And if we know that He hear us, whatsoever we ask, we know that we have the petitions that we desired if Him."   I John 5:14-15

Praise and Thanksgiving
"O Come, let us sing unto the LORD: let us make a joyful noise to the rock of our salvation . . . O come, let us worship and bow down: let us kneel before the LORD our Maker."   Psalm 95:1, 6

_____

_____

Repent through Confession
'Therefore say thou unto them, Thus saith the LORD of hosts; Turn ye unto Me, saith the LORD of hosts, and I will turn unto you, saith the LORD of hosts."   Zechariah 1:3

"Draw nigh to God, and He will draw nigh unto you. Cleanse your hands, ye sinners; and purify your hearts, ye double minded."   James 4:8

_____

_____

Ask
"Ask, and it shall be given you; seek, and you shall find; knock, and it shall be opened unto you: for everyone that asketh receiveth; and he that seeketh findeth; and to him that knocketh it shall be opened."

Matthew 7:7-8

Salvation

"For by grace are you saved through faith; . . . it is the gift of God"

Ephesians 2:8

Name	Date Entered	Date Answered

Yield to the Father (Prayer of surrender to the will of the Father)

"Nevertheless not what I will, but what thou wilt."   Mark 14:36b

Examine and Reflect

"Examine yourselves, whether ye be in faith; prove your own selves."

2 Corinthians 13:5

Notes

Date_____

"The effectual fervent prayer of a righteous man availeth much."

James 5:16b

Praise and Thanksgiving

"O Come, let us sing unto the LORD: let us make a joyful noise to the rock of our salvation . . . O come, let us worship and bow down: let us kneel before the LORD our Maker." Psalm 95:1, 6

_____

_____

Repent through Confession

'Therefore say thou unto them, Thus saith the LORD of hosts; Turn ye unto Me, saith the LORD of hosts, and I will turn unto you, saith the LORD of hosts." Zechariah 1:3

"Draw nigh to God, and He will draw nigh unto you. Cleanse your hands, ye sinners; and purify your hearts, ye double minded." James 4:8

_____

_____

Ask

"Therefore I say unto you, What things soever ye desire, when ye pray, believe that ye receive them, and ye shall have them" Mark 11:24

Church Leadership

"Finally, brethren, pray for us, that the word of the LORD may have free course, and be glorified, as as it is with you." 2 Thessalonians 3:1
"Behold, how good and how pleasant it is for the brethren to dwell together in unity." Psalm 133:1

Senior Pastor: (Personal) _____
(Professional) _____
Associate Pastor/Administrator: (Personal) _____
(Professional) _____
Associate Pastor/Music: (Personal) _____
(Professional) _____

Associate Pastor/Education: (Personal) _____
(Professional) _____
Children's Ministry Director: (Personal) _____
(Professional) _____
Other Ministerial Staff _____
Other Ministerial Staff _____
Other Ministerial Staff _____

Yield to the Father (Prayer of surrender to the will of the Father)
"Humble yourselves in the sight of the LORD, and He shall lift you up.

James 4:10

_____
_____

Examine and **R**eflect
"Examine me, O LORD, and prove me: . . ."   Psalm 26:2

_____
_____
_____
_____
_____
_____
_____

Date_____

"Let us therefore come boldly unto the throne of grace, that we may obtain mercy, and find grace to help in time of need.   Hebrews 4:16

Praise and Thanksgiving

"O Come, let us sing unto the LORD: let us make a joyful noise to the rock of our salvation . . . O come, let us worship and bow down: let us kneel before the LORD our Maker."   Psalm 95:1, 6

_____

_____

Repent through Confession

'Therefore say thou unto them, Thus saith the LORD of hosts; Turn ye unto Me, saith the LORD of hosts, and I will turn unto you, saith the LORD of hosts."   Zechariah 1:3

"Draw nigh to God, and He will draw nigh unto you. Cleanse your hands, ye sinners; and purify your hearts, ye double minded."   James 4:8

_____

_____

Ask

"If ye abide in Me, and my words abide in you, ye shall ask what ye will, and it shall be done unto you."   John 15:7

Government Leadership and Policy-makers

"I exhort therefore, that, first of all, supplications, prayers, intercessions, and giving of thanks be made for all men; for kings, and for all that are in authority; that we may lead a quiet and peaceable life in all godliness and honesty."

1 Timothy 2:1-3

National:_____

_____

_____

State:_____

_____

_____

Local_____

_____

_____

Yield to the Father (Prayer of surrender to the will of the Father)

"Obey them that have the rule over you, and submit yourselves: for they watch for your souls, as they that must give account, that they may do it with joy, and not with grief: for that is unprofitable for you."

Hebrews 13:17

_____

_____

_____

_____

_____

Examine and Reflect

"But let every man prove his own work, and then shall he have rejoicing in himself alone, and not in another." Galatians 6:4

_____

_____

_____

_____

_____

_____

Notes

_____

_____

_____

_____

_____

_____

_____

Date_____

"Call unto Me, and I will answer thee, and shew thee great and might things, which thou knowest not.   Jeremiah 33:3

Praise and Thanksgiving

"O Come, let us sing unto the Lord: let us make a joyful noise to the rock of our salvation . . . O come, let us worship and bow down: let us kneel before the Lord our Maker."   Psalm 95:1, 6

_____

_____

Repent through Confession

'Therefore say thou unto them, Thus saith the Lord of hosts; Turn ye unto Me, saith the Lord of hosts, and I will turn unto you, saith the Lord of hosts."   Zechariah 1:3

"Draw nigh to God, and He will draw nigh unto you. Cleanse your hands, ye sinners; and purify your hearts, ye double minded."   James 4:8

_____

_____

Ask

"And all things, whatsoever ye shall ask in prayer, believing, ye shall receive.   Matthew 21:22

Active Military members:

Name	Need	Date Entered	Date Answered

Missionaries

_____

_____

_____

_____

Yield to the Father (Prayer of surrender to the will of the Father)

"Nevertheless not what I will, but what thou wilt."　　　　Mark 14:36

_____

_____

_____

_____

_____

Examine and Reflect

"Examine yourselves, whether ye be in the faith; prove your own selves. Know ye not your own selves, how that Jesus Christ is in your, except ye be reprobates?　　　　2 Corinthians 13:5

_____

_____

_____

_____

_____

_____

Notes

_____

_____

_____

_____

_____

_____

_____

_____

_____

_____

_____

_____

_____

_____

_____

_____

_____

Date_____

"Now unto Him that is able to do exceeding abundantly above all that we ask or think, according to the power that worketh in us. Ephesians 3:20

Praise and Thanksgiving

"O Come, let us sing unto the LORD: let us make a joyful noise to the rock of our salvation . . . O come, let us worship and bow down: let us kneel before the LORD our Maker."   Psalm 95:1, 6

_____

_____

Repent through Confession

'Therefore say thou unto them, Thus saith the LORD of hosts; Turn ye unto Me, saith the LORD of hosts, and I will turn unto you, saith the LORD of hosts."   Zechariah 1:3

"Draw nigh to God, and He will draw nigh unto you. Cleanse your hands, ye sinners; and purify your hearts, ye double minded."   James 4:8

_____

_____

Ask

"As, and it shall be given you; seek, and you shall find; knock, and it shall be opened unto you: for everyone that asketh receiveth; and he that seeketh findeth; and to him that knocketh it shall be opened."

                                                      Matthew 7:7-8

Physically ill

"The prayer of faith shall save the sick, and the LORD shall raise him."

                                                        James 5:15

Name	Need	Date Entered	Date Answered

Yield to the Father (Prayer of surrender to the will of the Father)

"Know ye not, that to whom ye yield yourself servants to obey, his servants ye are to whom ye obey; whether of sin unto death, or of obedience unto righteousness?" Romans 6:16

_____

_____

_____

_____

_____

Examine and Reflect

"Search me, O God, and know my heart: try me, and know my thoughts. And see if there be any wicked way in me, and lead me in the way everlasting." Psalm 139:23-24

_____

_____

_____

_____

_____

Notes

_____

_____

_____

_____

_____

_____

_____

_____

_____

_____

_____

_____

_____

_____

Date_____

Praise and Thanksgiving
"O Come, let us sing unto the LORD: let us make a joyful noise to the rock
of our salvation . . . O come, let us worship and bow down: let us kneel
before the LORD our Maker."   Psalm 95:1, 6

_____

_____

Repent through Confession
'Therefore say thou unto them, Thus saith the LORD of hosts; Turn ye unto
Me, saith the LORD of hosts, and I will turn unto you, saith the LORD of
hosts."   Zechariah 1:3

"Draw nigh to God, and He will draw nigh unto you. Cleanse your hands,
ye sinners; and purify your hearts, ye double minded."   James 4:8

_____

_____

Ask
"But my God shall supply all your need according to His riches in glory
by Christ Jesus.   Philippians 4:19

Those with Relationship Problems:

Name	Need	Date Entered	Date Answered

Yield to the Father (**Prayer of surrender to the will of the Father**)
"Neither yield ye your members as instruments of unrighteousness unto sin: but yield yourselves unto God, as those that are alive from the dead, and your members as instruments of righteousness unto God."

Romans 6:13

_____
_____
_____
_____

Examine and **R**eflect
"Judge me, O Lord; for I have walked in my integrity; I have trusted also in the Lord; therefore I shall not slide."

Psalm 26:1

_____
_____
_____
_____
_____

Notes

_____
_____
_____
_____
_____
_____
_____
_____
_____
_____
_____
_____
_____
_____
_____

Date_____

"Beloved, if our heart condemn us not, then have we confidence toward God. And whatsoever we ask, we receive of Him, because we keep His commandments, and do those things that are pleasing in His sight.
1 John 3:21-22

Praise and Thanksgiving

"O Come, let us sing unto the LORD: let us make a joyful noise to the rock of our salvation . . . O come, let us worship and bow down: let us kneel before the LORD our Maker."
Psalm 95:1, 6

_____

_____

Repent through Confession

'Therefore say thou unto them, Thus saith the LORD of hosts; Turn ye unto Me, saith the LORD of hosts, and I will turn unto you, saith the LORD of hosts."
Zechariah 1:3

"Draw nigh to God, and He will draw nigh unto you. Cleanse your hands, ye sinners; and purify your hearts, ye double minded."
James 4:8

_____

_____

Ask

"And His disciples came to Him, and awoke Him, saying, LORD, save us: we perish. And He saith unto them, Why are ye fearful, O ye of little faith? Then He arose, and rebuked the winds and the sea; and there was great calm."
Matthew 8:26

"Likewise the Spirit also helpeth our infirmities: for we know not what we should pray for as we ought: but the Spirit itself maketh intercession for us with groanings which cannot be uttered."
Romans 8:26

Personal needs:	Date Entered	Date Answered

Personal desires for the glory of God:

_____

_____

(Yield to the Father) Prayer of surrender to the will of the Father
"Submit yourselves therefore to God. Resist the devil, and he will flee
from you."   James 4:7

_____

_____

_____

_____

Examine and Reflect
"Let my cry come near before The, O LORD: give me understanding
according to Thy word."   Psalm 119:169

_____

_____

_____

_____

_____

Notes

_____

_____

_____

_____

_____

_____

_____

_____

_____

_____

_____

_____

_____

Date_____

"He hears and answers every prayer, where the *true conditions* of praying are met." (*italics* inserted for emphasis)

E. M. Bounds, "The Possibilities of Prayer"

"And this is the confidence that we have in Him, that, if we ask anything according to His will, He heareth us: And if we know that He hear us, whatsoever we ask, we know that we have the petitions that we desired if Him." I John 5:14-15

Praise and Thanksgiving
"O Come, let us sing unto the LORD: let us make a joyful noise to the rock of our salvation . . . O come, let us worship and bow down: let us kneel before the LORD our Maker." Psalm 95:1, 6

_____

_____

Repent through Confession
'Therefore say thou unto them, Thus saith the LORD of hosts; Turn ye unto Me, saith the LORD of hosts, and I will turn unto you, saith the LORD of hosts." Zechariah 1:3

"Draw nigh to God, and He will draw nigh unto you. Cleanse your hands, ye sinners; and purify your hearts, ye double minded." James 4:8

_____

_____

Ask
"Ask, and it shall be given you; seek, and you shall find; knock, and it shall be opened unto you: for everyone that asketh receiveth; and he that seeketh findeth; and to him that knocketh it shall be opened." Matthew 7:7-8

Salvation

"For by grace are you saved through faith; . . . it is the gift of God"

Ephesians 2:8

Name	Date Entered	Date Answered

Yield to the Father (Prayer of surrender to the will of the Father)

"Nevertheless not what I will, but what thou wilt."   Mark 14:36b

_____

_____

_____

_____

Examine and **R**eflect

"Examine yourselves, whether ye be in faith; prove your own selves."

2 Corinthians 13:5

_____

_____

_____

_____

_____

_____

Notes

_____

_____

_____

_____

_____

_____

_____

_____

_____

_____

Date_____

"The effectual fervent prayer of a righteous man availeth much."

James 5:16b

Praise and Thanksgiving
"O Come, let us sing unto the LORD: let us make a joyful noise to the rock of our salvation . . . O come, let us worship and bow down: let us kneel before the LORD our Maker." Psalm 95:1, 6

_____

_____

Repent through Confession
'Therefore say thou unto them, Thus saith the LORD of hosts; Turn ye unto Me, saith the LORD of hosts, and I will turn unto you, saith the LORD of hosts." Zechariah 1:3

"Draw nigh to God, and He will draw nigh unto you. Cleanse your hands, ye sinners; and purify your hearts, ye double minded." James 4:8

_____

_____

Ask
"Therefore I say unto you, What things soever ye desire, when ye pray, believe that ye receive them, and ye shall have them" Mark 11:24

Church Leadership
"Finally, brethren, pray for us, that the word of the LORD may have free course, and be glorified, as as it is with you." 2 Thessalonians 3:1

"Behold, how good and how pleasant it is for the brethren to dwell together in unity." Psalm 133:1

Senior Pastor: (Personal) _____
(Professional) _____
Associate Pastor/Administrator: (Personal) _____
(Professional) _____

Associate Pastor/Music: (Personal) _____
(Professional) _____
Associate Pastor/Education: (Personal) _____
(Professional) _____
Children's Ministry Director: (Personal) _____
(Professional) _____
Other Ministerial Staff _____
Other Ministerial Staff _____
Other Ministerial Staff _____

Yield to the Father (Prayer of surrender to the will of the Father)
"Humble yourselves in the sight of the LORD, and He shall lift you up.
James 4:10

_____
_____
_____
_____

Examine and **R**eflect
"Examine me, O LORD, and prove me: . . ."   Psalm 26:2

_____
_____
_____
_____
_____

Notes

_____
_____
_____
_____
_____
_____
_____
_____
_____
_____
_____

Date_____

"Let us therefore come boldly unto the throne of grace, that we may obtain mercy, and find grace to help in time of need.   Hebrews 4:16

Praise and Thanksgiving
"O Come, let us sing unto the LORD: let us make a joyful noise to the rock of our salvation . . . O come, let us worship and bow down: let us kneel before the LORD our Maker."   Psalm 95:1, 6

_____

_____

Repent through Confession
'Therefore say thou unto them, Thus saith the LORD of hosts; Turn ye unto Me, saith the LORD of hosts, and I will turn unto you, saith the LORD of hosts."   Zechariah 1:3

"Draw nigh to God, and He will draw nigh unto you. Cleanse your hands, ye sinners; and purify your hearts, ye double minded."   James 4:8

_____

_____

Ask
"If ye abide in Me, and my words abide in you, ye shall ask what ye will, and it shall be done unto you."   John 15:7

Government Leadership and Policy-makers
"I exhort therefore, that, first of all, supplications, prayers, intercessions, and giving of thanks be made for all men; for kings, and for all that are in authority; that we may lead a quiet and peaceable life in all godliness and honesty."   1 Timothy 2:1-3

National:_____

_____

_____

State:_____
_____
_____

Local_____
_____
_____

Y̲ield to the Father (Prayer of surrender to the will of the Father)
"Obey them that have the rule over you, and submit yourselves: for they watch for your souls, as they that must give account, that they may do it with joy, and not with grief: for that is unprofitable for you."

Hebrews 13:17

_____
_____
_____
_____
_____

E̲xamine and R̲eflect
"But let every man prove his own work, and then shall he have rejoicing in himself alone, and not in another."

Galatians 6:4

_____
_____
_____
_____
_____
_____

Notes

_____
_____
_____
_____
_____
_____
_____

Date_____

"Call unto Me, and I will answer thee, and shew thee great and might things, which thou knowest not.   Jeremiah 33:3

Praise and Thanksgiving
"O Come, let us sing unto the LORD: let us make a joyful noise to the rock of our salvation . . . O come, let us worship and bow down: let us kneel before the LORD our Maker."   Psalm 95:1, 6

_____

_____

Repent through Confession
'Therefore say thou unto them, Thus saith the LORD of hosts; Turn ye unto Me, saith the LORD of hosts, and I will turn unto you, saith the LORD of hosts."   Zechariah 1:3

"Draw nigh to God, and He will draw nigh unto you. Cleanse your hands, ye sinners; and purify your hearts, ye double minded."   James 4:8

_____

_____

Ask
"And all things, whatsoever ye shall ask in prayer, believing, ye shall receive.   Matthew 21:22

Active Military members:

Name	Need	Date Entered	Date Answered

Missionaries

_____

_____

_____

_____

Yield to the Father (Prayer of surrender to the will of the Father)
"Nevertheless not what I will, but what thou wilt." Mark 14:36

_____

_____

_____

_____

_____

Examine and Reflect
"Examine yourselves, whether ye be in the faith; prove your own selves. Know ye not your own selves, how that Jesus Christ is in your, except ye be reprobates? 2 Corinthians 13:5

_____

_____

_____

_____

_____

_____

Notes

_____

_____

_____

_____

_____

_____

_____

_____

_____

_____

_____

_____

_____

_____

_____

_____

Date_____

"Now unto Him that is able to do exceeding abundantly above all that we ask or think, according to the power that worketh in us. Ephesians 3:20

Praise and Thanksgiving
"O Come, let us sing unto the LORD: let us make a joyful noise to the rock of our salvation . . . O come, let us worship and bow down: let us kneel before the LORD our Maker."   Psalm 95:1, 6

_____

_____

Repent through Confession
'Therefore say thou unto them, Thus saith the LORD of hosts; Turn ye unto Me, saith the LORD of hosts, and I will turn unto you, saith the LORD of hosts."   Zechariah 1:3

"Draw nigh to God, and He will draw nigh unto you. Cleanse your hands, ye sinners; and purify your hearts, ye double minded."   James 4:8

_____

_____

Ask
"As, and it shall be given you; seek, and you shall find; knock, and it shall be opened unto you: for everyone that asketh receiveth; and he that seeketh findeth; and to him that knocketh it shall be opened."
                                                        Matthew 7:7-8

Physically ill
"The prayer of faith shall save the sick, and the LORD shall raise him."
                                                          James 5:15

Name	Need	Date Entered	Date Answered

Yield to the Father (Prayer of surrender to the will of the Father)

"Know ye not, that to whom ye yield yourself servants to obey, his servants ye are to whom ye obey; whether of sin unto death, or of obedience unto righteousness?"   Romans 6:16

_____

_____

_____

_____

_____

Examine and Reflect

"Search me, O God, and know my heart: try me, and know my thoughts. And see if there be any wicked way in me, and lead me in the way everlasting."   Psalm 139:23-24

_____

_____

_____

_____

_____

Notes

_____

_____

_____

_____

_____

_____

_____

_____

_____

_____

_____

_____

_____

_____

Date_____

Praise and Thanksgiving

"O Come, let us sing unto the LORD: let us make a joyful noise to the rock of our salvation . . . O come, let us worship and bow down: let us kneel before the LORD our Maker."   Psalm 95:1, 6

_____

_____

Repent through Confession

'Therefore say thou unto them, Thus saith the LORD of hosts; Turn ye unto Me, saith the LORD of hosts, and I will turn unto you, saith the LORD of hosts."   Zechariah 1:3

"Draw nigh to God, and He will draw nigh unto you. Cleanse your hands, ye sinners; and purify your hearts, ye double minded."   James 4:8

_____

_____

Ask

"But my God shall supply all your need according to His riches in glory by Christ Jesus.   Philippians 4:19

Those with Relationship Problems:

Name	Need	Date Entered	Date Answered

Yield to the Father (Prayer of surrender to the will of the Father)
"Neither yield ye your members as instruments of unrighteousness unto sin: but yield yourselves unto God, as those that are alive from the dead, and your members as instruments of righteousness unto God."

Romans 6:13

_____

_____

_____

_____

Examine and Reflect
"Judge me, O LORD; for I have walked in my integrity; I have trusted also in the LORD; therefore I shall not slide." Psalm 26:1

_____

_____

_____

_____

_____

Notes

_____

_____

_____

_____

_____

_____

_____

_____

_____

_____

_____

_____

_____

_____

_____

Date_____

"Beloved, if our heart condemn us not, then have we confidence toward God. And whatsoever we ask, we receive of Him, because we keep His command-ments, and do those things that are pleasing in His sight.
1 John 3:21-22

Praise and Thanksgiving
"O Come, let us sing unto the LORD: let us make a joyful noise to the rock of our salvation . . . O come, let us worship and bow down: let us kneel before the LORD our Maker."
Psalm 95:1, 6

_____

_____

Repent through Confession
'Therefore say thou unto them, Thus saith the LORD of hosts; Turn ye unto Me, saith the LORD of hosts, and I will turn unto you, saith the LORD of hosts."
Zechariah 1:3

"Draw nigh to God, and He will draw nigh unto you. Cleanse your hands, ye sinners; and purify your hearts, ye double minded."
James 4:8

_____

_____

Ask
"And His disciples came to Him, and awoke Him, saying, LORD, save us: we perish. And He saith unto them, Why are ye fearful, O ye of little faith? Then He arose, and rebuked the winds and the sea; and there was great calm."
Matthew 8:26
"Likewise the Spirit also helpeth our infirmities: for we know not what we should pray for as we ought: but the Spirit itself maketh intercession for us with groanings which cannot be uttered."
Romans 8:26

Personal needs: **Date Entered**   **Date Answered**

_____

_____

_____

Personal desires for the glory of God:

_____

_____

(Yield to the Father) Prayer of surrender to the will of the Father
"Submit yourselves therefore to God. Resist the devil, and he will flee from you." James 4:7

_____

_____

_____

_____

_____

Examine and Reflect
"Let my cry come near before The, O LORD: give me understanding according to Thy word." Psalm 119:169

_____

_____

_____

_____

_____

_____

Notes

_____

_____

_____

_____

_____

_____

_____

_____

_____

_____

_____

Date_____

"He hears and answers every prayer, where the *true conditions* of praying are met." (*italics* inserted for emphasis)

E. M. Bounds, "The Possibilities of Prayer"

"And this is the confidence that we have in Him, that, if we ask anything according to His will, He heareth us: And if we know that He hear us, whatsoever we ask, we know that we have the petitions that we desired if Him."
I John 5:14-15

Praise and Thanksgiving
"O Come, let us sing unto the LORD: let us make a joyful noise to the rock of our salvation . . . O come, let us worship and bow down: let us kneel before the LORD our Maker."
Psalm 95:1, 6

_____

_____

Repent through Confession
'Therefore say thou unto them, Thus saith the LORD of hosts; Turn ye unto Me, saith the LORD of hosts, and I will turn unto you, saith the LORD of hosts."
Zechariah 1:3

"Draw nigh to God, and He will draw nigh unto you. Cleanse your hands, ye sinners; and purify your hearts, ye double minded."
James 4:8

_____

_____

Ask
"Ask, and it shall be given you; seek, and you shall find; knock, and it shall be opened unto you: for everyone that asketh receiveth; and he that seeketh findeth; and to him that knocketh it shall be opened."
Matthew 7:7-8

Salvation

"For by grace are you saved through faith; . . . it is the gift of God"

Ephesians 2:8

Name	Date Entered	Date Answered

Yield to the Father (Prayer of surrender to the will of the Father)

"Nevertheless not what I will, but what thou wilt."   Mark 14:36b

_____

_____

_____

_____

Examine and Reflect

"Examine yourselves, whether ye be in faith; prove your own selves."

2 Corinthians 13:5

_____

_____

_____

_____

_____

_____

Notes

_____

_____

_____

_____

_____

_____

_____

_____

_____

Date_____

"The effectual fervent prayer of a righteous man availeth much."

James 5:16b

Praise and Thanksgiving
"O Come, let us sing unto the LORD: let us make a joyful noise to the rock of our salvation . . . O come, let us worship and bow down: let us kneel before the LORD our Maker." Psalm 95:1, 6

_____

_____

Repent through Confession
'Therefore say thou unto them, Thus saith the LORD of hosts; Turn ye unto Me, saith the LORD of hosts, and I will turn unto you, saith the LORD of hosts." Zechariah 1:3

"Draw nigh to God, and He will draw nigh unto you. Cleanse your hands, ye sinners; and purify your hearts, ye double minded." James 4:8

_____

_____

Ask
"Therefore I say unto you, What things soever ye desire, when ye pray, believe that ye receive them, and ye shall have them" Mark 11:24

Church Leadership
"Finally, brethren, pray for us, that the word of the LORD may have free course, and be glorified, as as it is with you." 2 Thessalonians 3:1

"Behold, how good and how pleasant it is for the brethren to dwell together in unity." Psalm 133:1

Senior Pastor: (Personal) _____
(Professional) _____
Associate Pastor/Administrator: (Personal) _____
(Professional) _____

Associate Pastor/Music: (Personal) _____

(Professional) _____

Associate Pastor/Education: (Personal) _____

(Professional) _____

Children's Ministry Director: (Personal) _____

(Professional) _____

Other Ministerial Staff _____

Other Ministerial Staff _____

Other Ministerial Staff _____

Yield to the Father (**Prayer of surrender to the will of the Father**)

"Humble yourselves in the sight of the LORD, and He shall lift you up.

James 4:10

_____

_____

_____

_____

Examine and **R**eflect

"Examine me, O LORD, and prove me: . . ."   Psalm 26:2

_____

_____

_____

_____

_____

_____

_____

_____

Date_____

"Let us therefore come boldly unto the throne of grace, that we may obtain mercy, and find grace to help in time of need.   Hebrews 4:16

Praise and Thanksgiving

"O Come, let us sing unto the LORD: let us make a joyful noise to the rock of our salvation . . . O come, let us worship and bow down: let us kneel before the LORD our Maker."   Psalm 95:1, 6

_____

_____

Repent through Confession

'Therefore say thou unto them, Thus saith the LORD of hosts; Turn ye unto Me, saith the LORD of hosts, and I will turn unto you, saith the LORD of hosts."   Zechariah 1:3

"Draw nigh to God, and He will draw nigh unto you. Cleanse your hands, ye sinners; and purify your hearts, ye double minded."   James 4:8

_____

_____

Ask

"If ye abide in Me, and my words abide in you, ye shall ask what ye will, and it shall be done unto you."   John 15:7

Government Leadership and Policy-makers

"I exhort therefore, that, first of all, supplications, prayers, intercessions, and giving of thanks be made for all men; for kings, and for all that are in authority; that we may lead a quiet and peaceable life in all godliness and honesty."   1 Timothy 2:1-3

National:_____

_____

_____

State:_____

_____

_____

Local_____

_____

_____

Yield to the Father (Prayer of surrender to the will of the Father)
"Obey them that have the rule over you, and submit yourselves: for they watch for your souls, as they that must give account, that they may do it with joy, and not with grief: for that is unprofitable for you."

Hebrews 13:17

_____

_____

_____

_____

_____

Examine and Reflect
"But let every man prove his own work, and then shall he have rejoicing in himself alone, and not in another." Galatians 6:4

_____

_____

_____

_____

_____

Notes

_____

_____

_____

_____

_____

_____

_____

Date_____

"Call unto Me, and I will answer thee, and shew thee great and might things, which thou knowest not. Jeremiah 33:3

Praise and Thanksgiving

"O Come, let us sing unto the LORD: let us make a joyful noise to the rock of our salvation . . . O come, let us worship and bow down: let us kneel before the LORD our Maker." Psalm 95:1, 6

_____

_____

Repent through Confession

'Therefore say thou unto them, Thus saith the LORD of hosts; Turn ye unto Me, saith the LORD of hosts, and I will turn unto you, saith the LORD of hosts." Zechariah 1:3

"Draw nigh to God, and He will draw nigh unto you. Cleanse your hands, ye sinners; and purify your hearts, ye double minded." James 4:8

_____

_____

Ask

"And all things, whatsoever ye shall ask in prayer, believing, ye shall receive. Matthew 21:22

Active Military members:

Name	Need	Date Entered	Date Answered

Missionaries

_____

_____

_____

_____

Yield to the Father (Prayer of surrender to the will of the Father)
"Nevertheless not what I will, but what thou wilt."   Mark 14:36

_____
_____
_____
_____
_____

Examine and Reflect
"Examine yourselves, whether ye be in the faith; prove your own selves.
Know ye not your own selves, how that Jesus Christ is in your, except ye
be reprobates?   2 Corinthians 13:5

_____
_____
_____
_____
_____
_____

Notes

_____
_____
_____
_____
_____
_____
_____
_____
_____
_____
_____
_____
_____
_____
_____
_____
_____

Date_____

"Now unto Him that is able to do exceeding abundantly above all that we ask or think, according to the power that worketh in us. Ephesians 3:20

Praise and Thanksgiving

"O Come, let us sing unto the LORD: let us make a joyful noise to the rock of our salvation . . . O come, let us worship and bow down: let us kneel before the LORD our Maker."   Psalm 95:1, 6

_____

_____

Repent through Confession

'Therefore say thou unto them, Thus saith the LORD of hosts; Turn ye unto Me, saith the LORD of hosts, and I will turn unto you, saith the LORD of hosts."   Zechariah 1:3

"Draw nigh to God, and He will draw nigh unto you. Cleanse your hands, ye sinners; and purify your hearts, ye double minded."   James 4:8

_____

_____

Ask

"As, and it shall be given you; seek, and you shall find; knock, and it shall be opened unto you: for everyone that asketh receiveth; and he that seeketh findeth; and to him that knocketh it shall be opened."
                                                                        Matthew 7:7-8

Physically ill
"The prayer of faith shall save the sick, and the LORD shall raise him."
                                                                        James 5:15

Name	Need	Date Entered	Date Answered

Yield to the Father (Prayer of surrender to the will of the Father)
"Know ye not, that to whom ye yield yourself servants to obey, his servants ye are to whom ye obey; whether of sin unto death, or of obedience unto righteousness?"

Romans 6:16

_____

_____

_____

_____

_____

Examine and Reflect
"Search me, O God, and know my heart: try me, and know my thoughts. And see if there be any wicked way in me, and lead me in the way everlasting."

Psalm 139:23-24

_____

_____

_____

_____

_____

Notes

_____

_____

_____

_____

_____

_____

_____

_____

_____

_____

_____

_____

Date_____

"... the will of the LORD be done."   Acts 21:14

Praise and Thanksgiving
"O Come, let us sing unto the LORD: let us make a joyful noise to the rock
of our salvation . . . O come, let us worship and bow down: let us kneel
before the LORD our Maker."   Psalm 95:1, 6

_____

_____

Repent through Confession
'Therefore say thou unto them, Thus saith the LORD of hosts; Turn ye unto
Me, saith the LORD of hosts, and I will turn unto you, saith the LORD of
hosts."   Zechariah 1:3

"Draw nigh to God, and He will draw nigh unto you. Cleanse your hands,
ye sinners; and purify your hearts, ye double minded."   James 4:8

_____

_____

Ask
"But my God shall supply all your need according to His riches in glory
by Christ Jesus.   Philippians 4:19

Those with Relationship Problems:

Name	Need	Date Entered	Date Answered

Yield to the Father (Prayer of surrender to the will of the Father)

"Neither yield ye your members as instruments of unrighteousness unto sin: but yield yourselves unto God, as those that are alive from the dead, and your members as instruments of righteousness unto God."

Romans 6:13

_____

_____

_____

_____

Examine and Reflect

"Judge me, O LORD; for I have walked in my integrity; I have trusted also in the LORD; therefore I shall not slide." Psalm 26:1

_____

_____

_____

_____

_____

_____

Notes

_____

_____

_____

_____

_____

_____

_____

_____

_____

_____

_____

_____

_____

_____

_____

_____

Date_____

"Beloved, if our heart condemn us not, then have we confidence toward God. And whatsoever we ask, we receive of Him, because we keep His command-ments, and do those things that are pleasing in His sight.

1 John 3:21-22

Praise and Thanksgiving

"O Come, let us sing unto the LORD: let us make a joyful noise to the rock of our salvation . . . O come, let us worship and bow down: let us kneel before the LORD our Maker."

Psalm 95:1, 6

_____

_____

Repent through Confession

'Therefore say thou unto them, Thus saith the LORD of hosts; Turn ye unto Me, saith the LORD of hosts, and I will turn unto you, saith the LORD of hosts."

Zechariah 1:3

"Draw nigh to God, and He will draw nigh unto you. Cleanse your hands, ye sinners; and purify your hearts, ye double minded."

James 4:8

_____

_____

Ask

"And His disciples came to Him, and awoke Him, saying, LORD, save us: we perish. And He saith unto them, Why are ye fearful, O ye of little faith? Then He arose, and rebuked the winds and the sea; and there was great calm."

Matthew 8:26

"Likewise the Spirit also helpeth our infirmities: for we know not what we should pray for as we ought: but the Spirit itself maketh intercession for us with groanings which cannot be uttered."

Romans 8:26

Personal needs: **Date Entered**   **Date Answered**

_____

_____

Personal desires for the glory of God:

_____

_____

(Yield to the Father) Prayer of surrender to the will of the Father
"Submit yourselves therefore to God. Resist the devil, and he will flee
from you."   James 4:7

_____

_____

_____

_____

_____

Examine and Reflect
"Let my cry come near before The, O LORD: give me understanding
according to Thy word."   Psalm 119:169

_____

_____

_____

_____

_____

Notes

_____

_____

_____

_____

_____

_____

_____

_____

_____

_____

_____

Date_____

"He hears and answers every prayer, where the *true conditions* of praying are met." (*italics* inserted for emphasis)

E. M. Bounds, "The Possibilities of Prayer"

"And this is the confidence that we have in Him, that, if we ask anything according to His will, He heareth us: And if we know that He hear us, whatsoever we ask, we know that we have the petitions that we desired if Him."

I John 5:14-15

Praise and Thanksgiving

"O Come, let us sing unto the LORD: let us make a joyful noise to the rock of our salvation . . . O come, let us worship and bow down: let us kneel before the LORD our Maker."

Psalm 95:1, 6

_____

_____

Repent through Confession

'Therefore say thou unto them, Thus saith the LORD of hosts; Turn ye unto Me, saith the LORD of hosts, and I will turn unto you, saith the LORD of hosts."

Zechariah 1:3

"Draw nigh to God, and He will draw nigh unto you. Cleanse your hands, ye sinners; and purify your hearts, ye double minded."

James 4:8

_____

_____

Ask

"Ask, and it shall be given you; seek, and you shall find; knock, and it shall be opened unto you: for everyone that asketh receiveth; and he that seeketh findeth; and to him that knocketh it shall be opened."

Matthew 7:7-8

Salvation

"For by grace are you saved through faith; . . . it is the gift of God"

Ephesians 2:8

Name   **Date Entered**   **Date Answered**

_____

_____

_____

Yield to the Father (Prayer of surrender to the will of the Father)

"Nevertheless not what I will, but what thou wilt."   Mark 14:36b

_____

_____

_____

_____

Examine and Reflect

"Examine yourselves, whether ye be in faith; prove your own selves."

2 Corinthians 13:5

_____

_____

_____

_____

_____

_____

Notes

_____

_____

_____

_____

_____

_____

_____

_____

_____

Date_____

"The effectual fervent prayer of a righteous man availeth much."

James 5:16b

Praise and Thanksgiving

"O Come, let us sing unto the LORD: let us make a joyful noise to the rock of our salvation . . . O come, let us worship and bow down: let us kneel before the LORD our Maker."

Psalm 95:1, 6

_____

_____

Repent through Confession

'Therefore say thou unto them, Thus saith the LORD of hosts; Turn ye unto Me, saith the LORD of hosts, and I will turn unto you, saith the LORD of hosts."

Zechariah 1:3

"Draw nigh to God, and He will draw nigh unto you. Cleanse your hands, ye sinners; and purify your hearts, ye double minded."

James 4:8

_____

_____

Ask

"Therefore I say unto you, What things soever ye desire, when ye pray, believe that ye receive them, and ye shall have them"

Mark 11:24

Church Leadership

"Finally, brethren, pray for us, that the word of the LORD may have free course, and be glorified, as as it is with you."

2 Thessalonians 3:1

"Behold, how good and how pleasant it is for the brethren to dwell together in unity."

Psalm 133:1

Senior Pastor: (Personal) _____

(Professional) _____

Associate Pastor/Administrator: (Personal) _____

(Professional) _____

Associate Pastor/Music: (Personal) _____
(Professional) _____
Associate Pastor/Education: (Personal) _____
(Professional) _____
Children's Ministry Director: (Personal) _____
(Professional) _____
Other Ministerial Staff _____
Other Ministerial Staff _____
Other Ministerial Staff _____

Yield to the Father (Prayer of surrender to the will of the Father)
"Humble yourselves in the sight of the LORD, and He shall lift you up.
James 4:10

_____
_____
_____
_____

Examine and Reflect
"Examine me, O LORD, and prove me: . . ."   Psalm 26:2

_____
_____
_____
_____
_____
_____
_____
_____

Date_____

"Let us therefore come boldly unto the throne of grace, that we may obtain mercy, and find grace to help in time of need.   Hebrews 4:16

Praise and Thanksgiving
"O Come, let us sing unto the LORD: let us make a joyful noise to the rock of our salvation . . . O come, let us worship and bow down: let us kneel before the LORD our Maker."   Psalm 95:1, 6

_____

_____

Repent through Confession
'Therefore say thou unto them, Thus saith the LORD of hosts; Turn ye unto Me, saith the LORD of hosts, and I will turn unto you, saith the LORD of hosts."   Zechariah 1:3

"Draw nigh to God, and He will draw nigh unto you. Cleanse your hands, ye sinners; and purify your hearts, ye double minded."   James 4:8

_____

_____

Ask
"If ye abide in Me, and my words abide in you, ye shall ask what ye will, and it shall be done unto you."   John 15:7

Government Leadership and Policy-makers
"I exhort therefore, that, first of all, supplications, prayers, intercessions, and giving of thanks be made for all men; for kings, and for all that are in authority; that we may lead a quiet and peaceable life in all godliness and honesty."   1 Timothy 2:1-3

National:_____

_____

_____

State:_____

_____

_____

Local_____

_____

_____

<u>Y</u>ield to the Father (Prayer of surrender to the will of the Father)

"Obey them that have the rule over you, and submit yourselves: for they watch for your souls, as they that must give account, that they may do it with joy, and not with grief: for that is unprofitable for you."

Hebrews 13:17

_____

_____

_____

_____

_____

<u>E</u>xamine and <u>R</u>eflect

"But let every man prove his own work, and then shall he have rejoicing in himself alone, and not in another." Galatians 6:4

_____

_____

_____

_____

_____

_____

Notes

_____

_____

_____

_____

_____

_____

_____

Date_____

"Call unto Me, and I will answer thee, and shew thee great and might things, which thou knowest not.   Jeremiah 33:3

Praise and Thanksgiving
"O Come, let us sing unto the LORD: let us make a joyful noise to the rock of our salvation . . . O come, let us worship and bow down: let us kneel before the LORD our Maker."   Psalm 95:1, 6

_____

_____

Repent through Confession
'Therefore say thou unto them, Thus saith the LORD of hosts; Turn ye unto Me, saith the LORD of hosts, and I will turn unto you, saith the LORD of hosts."   Zechariah 1:3

"Draw nigh to God, and He will draw nigh unto you. Cleanse your hands, ye sinners; and purify your hearts, ye double minded."   James 4:8

_____

_____

Ask
"And all things, whatsoever ye shall ask in prayer, believing, ye shall receive.   Matthew 21:22

Active Military members:

Name	Need	Date Entered	Date Answered

Missionaries

_____

_____

_____

_____

Yield to the Father (Prayer of surrender to the will of the Father)
"Nevertheless not what I will, but what thou wilt."   Mark 14:36

_____
_____
_____
_____
_____

Examine and Reflect
"Examine yourselves, whether ye be in the faith; prove your own selves.
Know ye not your own selves, how that Jesus Christ is in your, except ye
be reprobates?   2 Corinthians 13:5

_____
_____
_____
_____
_____
_____

Notes

_____
_____
_____
_____
_____
_____
_____
_____
_____
_____
_____
_____
_____
_____
_____

Date_____

"Now unto Him that is able to do exceeding abundantly above all that we ask or think, according to the power that worketh in us. Ephesians 3:20

Praise and Thanksgiving
"O Come, let us sing unto the LORD: let us make a joyful noise to the rock of our salvation . . . O come, let us worship and bow down: let us kneel before the LORD our Maker."   Psalm 95:1, 6

_____

_____

Repent through Confession
'Therefore say thou unto them, Thus saith the LORD of hosts; Turn ye unto Me, saith the LORD of hosts, and I will turn unto you, saith the LORD of hosts."   Zechariah 1:3

"Draw nigh to God, and He will draw nigh unto you. Cleanse your hands, ye sinners; and purify your hearts, ye double minded."   James 4:8

_____

_____

Ask
"As, and it shall be given you; seek, and you shall find; knock, and it shall be opened unto you: for everyone that asketh receiveth; and he that seeketh findeth; and to him that knocketh it shall be opened."
                                                        Matthew 7:7-8

Physically ill
"The prayer of faith shall save the sick, and the LORD shall raise him."
                                                        James 5:15

Name	Need	Date Entered	Date Answered

Yield to the Father (Prayer of surrender to the will of the Father)

"Know ye not, that to whom ye yield yourself servants to obey, his servants ye are to whom ye obey; whether of sin unto death, or of obedience unto righteousness?"   Romans 6:16

_____

_____

_____

_____

_____

Examine and Reflect

"Search me, O God, and know my heart: try me, and know my thoughts. And see if there be any wicked way in me, and lead me in the way everlasting."   Psalm 139:23-24

_____

_____

_____

_____

_____

Notes

_____

_____

_____

_____

_____

_____

_____

_____

_____

_____

_____

_____

_____

_____

Date_____

". . . the will of the LORD be done."   Acts 21:14

Praise and Thanksgiving
"O Come, let us sing unto the LORD: let us make a joyful noise to the rock
of our salvation . . . O come, let us worship and bow down: let us kneel
before the LORD our Maker."   Psalm 95:1, 6

_____

_____

Repent through Confession
'Therefore say thou unto them, Thus saith the LORD of hosts; Turn ye unto
Me, saith the LORD of hosts, and I will turn unto you, saith the LORD of
hosts."   Zechariah 1:3

"Draw nigh to God, and He will draw nigh unto you. Cleanse your hands,
ye sinners; and purify your hearts, ye double minded."   James 4:8

_____

_____

Ask
"But my God shall supply all your need according to His riches in glory
by Christ Jesus.   Philippians 4:19

Those with Relationship Problems:

Name	Need	Date Entered	Date Answered

<u>Y</u>ield to the Father (Prayer of surrender to the will of the Father)

"Neither yield ye your members as instruments of unrighteousness unto sin: but yield yourselves unto God, as those that are alive from the dead, and your members as instruments of righteousness unto God."

Romans 6:13

_____
_____
_____
_____

<u>E</u>xamine and <u>R</u>eflect

"Judge me, O LORD; for I have walked in my integrity; I have trusted also in the LORD; therefore I shall not slide." Psalm 26:1

_____
_____
_____
_____
_____

Notes

_____
_____
_____
_____
_____
_____
_____
_____
_____
_____
_____
_____
_____
_____

Date_____

"Beloved, if our heart condemn us not, then have we confidence toward God. And whatsoever we ask, we receive of Him, because we keep His command-ments, and do those things that are pleasing in His sight.
1 John 3:21-22

Praise and Thanksgiving
"O Come, let us sing unto the LORD: let us make a joyful noise to the rock of our salvation . . . O come, let us worship and bow down: let us kneel before the LORD our Maker." Psalm 95:1, 6

_____

_____

Repent through Confession
'Therefore say thou unto them, Thus saith the LORD of hosts; Turn ye unto Me, saith the LORD of hosts, and I will turn unto you, saith the LORD of hosts." Zechariah 1:3

"Draw nigh to God, and He will draw nigh unto you. Cleanse your hands, ye sinners; and purify your hearts, ye double minded." James 4:8

_____

_____

Ask
"And His disciples came to Him, and awoke Him, saying, LORD, save us: we perish. And He saith unto them, Why are ye fearful, O ye of little faith? Then He arose, and rebuked the winds and the sea; and there was great calm." Matthew 8:26

"Likewise the Spirit also helpeth our infirmities: for we know not what we should pray for as we ought: but the Spirit itself maketh intercession for us with groanings which cannot be uttered." Romans 8:26

Personal needs: **Date Entered**   **Date Answered**

_____

_____

Personal desires for the glory of God:

_____

_____

(Yield to the Father) Prayer of surrender to the will of the Father
"Submit yourselves therefore to God. Resist the devil, and he will flee
from you."   James 4:7

_____

_____

_____

_____

_____

Examine and Reflect
"Let my cry come near before The, O LORD: give me understanding
according to Thy word."   Psalm 119:169

_____

_____

_____

_____

_____

_____

_____

Notes

_____

_____

_____

_____

_____

_____

_____

_____

_____

Date_____

"He hears and answers every prayer, where the *true conditions* of praying are met." (*italics* inserted for emphasis)

E. M. Bounds, "The Possibilities of Prayer"

"And this is the confidence that we have in Him, that, if we ask anything according to His will, He heareth us: And if we know that He hear us, whatsoever we ask, we know that we have the petitions that we desired if Him."

I John 5:14-15

Praise and Thanksgiving

"O Come, let us sing unto the LORD: let us make a joyful noise to the rock of our salvation . . . O come, let us worship and bow down: let us kneel before the LORD our Maker."

Psalm 95:1, 6

_____

_____

Repent through Confession

'Therefore say thou unto them, Thus saith the LORD of hosts; Turn ye unto Me, saith the LORD of hosts, and I will turn unto you, saith the LORD of hosts."

Zechariah 1:3

"Draw nigh to God, and He will draw nigh unto you. Cleanse your hands, ye sinners; and purify your hearts, ye double minded." James 4:8

_____

_____

Ask

"Ask, and it shall be given you; seek, and you shall find; knock, and it shall be opened unto you: for everyone that asketh receiveth; and he that seeketh findeth; and to him that knocketh it shall be opened."

Matthew 7:7-8

Salvation

"For by grace are you saved through faith; . . . it is the gift of God"

Ephesians 2:8

Name   **Date Entered**   **Date Answered**

_____

_____

_____

<u>Y</u>ield **to the Father (Prayer of surrender to the will of the Father)**

"Nevertheless not what I will, but what thou wilt."   Mark 14:36b

_____

_____

_____

_____

<u>E</u>xamine and <u>R</u>eflect

"Examine yourselves, whether ye be in faith; prove your own selves."

2 Corinthians 13:5

_____

_____

_____

_____

_____

_____

Date_____

"The effectual fervent prayer of a righteous man availeth much."

James 5:16b

Praise and Thanksgiving

"O Come, let us sing unto the LORD: let us make a joyful noise to the rock of our salvation . . . O come, let us worship and bow down: let us kneel before the LORD our Maker." Psalm 95:1, 6

_____

_____

Repent through Confession

'Therefore say thou unto them, Thus saith the LORD of hosts; Turn ye unto Me, saith the LORD of hosts, and I will turn unto you, saith the LORD of hosts." Zechariah 1:3

"Draw nigh to God, and He will draw nigh unto you. Cleanse your hands, ye sinners; and purify your hearts, ye double minded." James 4:8

_____

_____

Ask

"Therefore I say unto you, What things soever ye desire, when ye pray, believe that ye receive them, and ye shall have them" Mark 11:24

Church Leadership

"Finally, brethren, pray for us, that the word of the LORD may have free course, and be glorified, as as it is with you." 2 Thessalonians 3:1

"Behold, how good and how pleasant it is for the brethren to dwell together in unity." Psalm 133:1

Senior Pastor: (Personal) _____
(Professional) _____
Associate Pastor/Administrator: (Personal) _____
(Professional) _____

Associate Pastor/Music: (Personal) _____
(Professional) _____
Associate Pastor/Education: (Personal) _____
(Professional) _____
Children's Ministry Director: (Personal) _____
(Professional) _____
Other Ministerial Staff _____
Other Ministerial Staff _____
Other Ministerial Staff _____

Yield to the Father (Prayer of surrender to the will of the Father)
"Humble yourselves in the sight of the LORD, and He shall lift you up.

James 4:10

_____
_____
_____
_____

Examine and Reflect
"Examine me, O LORD, and prove me: . . ."   Psalm 26:2

_____
_____
_____
_____
_____
_____
_____

Date_____

"Let us therefore come boldly unto the throne of grace, that we may obtain mercy, and find grace to help in time of need.   Hebrews 4:16

Praise and Thanksgiving

"O Come, let us sing unto the LORD: let us make a joyful noise to the rock of our salvation . . . O come, let us worship and bow down: let us kneel before the LORD our Maker."   Psalm 95:1, 6

_____

_____

Repent through Confession

'Therefore say thou unto them, Thus saith the LORD of hosts; Turn ye unto Me, saith the LORD of hosts, and I will turn unto you, saith the LORD of hosts."   Zechariah 1:3

"Draw nigh to God, and He will draw nigh unto you. Cleanse your hands, ye sinners; and purify your hearts, ye double minded."   James 4:8

_____

_____

Ask

"If ye abide in Me, and my words abide in you, ye shall ask what ye will, and it shall be done unto you."   John 15:7

Government Leadership and Policy-makers

"I exhort therefore, that, first of all, supplications, prayers, intercessions, and giving of thanks be made for all men; for kings, and for all that are in authority; that we may lead a quiet and peaceable life in all godliness and honesty."

1 Timothy 2:1-3

National:_____

_____

_____

State:_____

_____

_____

Local_____

_____

_____

Y̲ield to the Father (Prayer of surrender to the will of the Father)
"Obey them that have the rule over you, and submit yourselves: for they watch for your souls, as they that must give account, that they may do it with joy, and not with grief: for that is unprofitable for you."

Hebrews 13:17

_____

_____

_____

_____

_____

E̲xamine and R̲eflect
"But let every man prove his own work, and then shall he have rejoicing in himself alone, and not in another." Galatians 6:4

_____

_____

_____

_____

_____

_____

Notes

_____

_____

_____

_____

_____

Date_____

"Call unto Me, and I will answer thee, and shew thee great and might things, which thou knowest not.   Jeremiah 33:3

Praise and Thanksgiving
"O Come, let us sing unto the LORD: let us make a joyful noise to the rock of our salvation . . . O come, let us worship and bow down: let us kneel before the LORD our Maker."   Psalm 95:1, 6

_____

_____

Repent through Confession
'Therefore say thou unto them, Thus saith the LORD of hosts; Turn ye unto Me, saith the LORD of hosts, and I will turn unto you, saith the LORD of hosts."   Zechariah 1:3

"Draw nigh to God, and He will draw nigh unto you. Cleanse your hands, ye sinners; and purify your hearts, ye double minded."   James 4:8

_____

_____

Ask
"And all things, whatsoever ye shall ask in prayer, believing, ye shall receive.   Matthew 21:22

Active Military members:
Name	Need	Date Entered	Date Answered

Missionaries
_____

_____

_____

_____

Yield to the Father (Prayer of surrender to the will of the Father)

"Nevertheless not what I will, but what thou wilt."   Mark 14:36

_____

_____

_____

_____

_____

Examine and Reflect

"Examine yourselves, whether ye be in the faith; prove your own selves. Know ye not your own selves, how that Jesus Christ is in your, except ye be reprobates?   2 Corinthians 13:5

_____

_____

_____

_____

_____

Notes

_____

_____

_____

_____

_____

_____

_____

_____

_____

_____

_____

_____

_____

_____

_____

Date_____

"Now unto Him that is able to do exceeding abundantly above all that we ask or think, according to the power that worketh in us. Ephesians 3:20

Praise and Thanksgiving

"O Come, let us sing unto the LORD: let us make a joyful noise to the rock of our salvation . . . O come, let us worship and bow down: let us kneel before the LORD our Maker."   Psalm 95:1, 6

_____

_____

Repent through Confession

'Therefore say thou unto them, Thus saith the LORD of hosts; Turn ye unto Me, saith the LORD of hosts, and I will turn unto you, saith the LORD of hosts."   Zechariah 1:3

"Draw nigh to God, and He will draw nigh unto you. Cleanse your hands, ye sinners; and purify your hearts, ye double minded."   James 4:8

_____

_____

Ask

"As, and it shall be given you; seek, and you shall find; knock, and it shall be opened unto you: for everyone that asketh receiveth; and he that seeketh findeth; and to him that knocketh it shall be opened."

Matthew 7:7-8

Physically ill

"The prayer of faith shall save the sick, and the LORD shall raise him."

James 5:15

Name	Need	Date Entered	Date Answered

Yield to the Father (Prayer of surrender to the will of the Father)

"Know ye not, that to whom ye yield yourself servants to obey, his servants ye are to whom ye obey; whether of sin unto death, or of obedience unto righteousness?"   Romans 6:16

_____

_____

_____

_____

_____

Examine and Reflect

"Search me, O God, and know my heart: try me, and know my thoughts. And see if there be any wicked way in me, and lead me in the way everlasting."

Psalm 139:23-24

_____

_____

_____

_____

_____

Notes

_____

_____

_____

_____

_____

_____

_____

_____

_____

_____

_____

_____

_____

_____

Date_____

". . . the will of the LORD be done."   Acts 21:14

Praise and Thanksgiving
"O Come, let us sing unto the LORD: let us make a joyful noise to the rock of our salvation . . . O come, let us worship and bow down: let us kneel before the LORD our Maker."   Psalm 95:1, 6

_____

_____

Repent through Confession
'Therefore say thou unto them, Thus saith the LORD of hosts; Turn ye unto Me, saith the LORD of hosts, and I will turn unto you, saith the LORD of hosts."   Zechariah 1:3

"Draw nigh to God, and He will draw nigh unto you. Cleanse your hands, ye sinners; and purify your hearts, ye double minded."   James 4:8

_____

_____

Ask
"But my God shall supply all your need according to His riches in glory by Christ Jesus.   Philippians 4:19

Those with Relationship Problems:

Name	Need	Date Entered	Date Answered

(Yield to the Father) Prayer of surrender to the will of the Father
"Nevertheless not what I will, but what thou wilt."   Mark 14:36 KJV

_____
_____
_____
_____
_____

Examine and Reflect   Galatians 6:1-5

_____
_____
_____
_____
_____
_____
_____

Notes

_____
_____
_____
_____
_____
_____
_____
_____
_____
_____
_____
_____
_____
_____
_____
_____
_____
_____

Date_____

"Beloved, if our heart condemn us not, then have we confidence toward God. And whatsoever we ask, we receive of Him, because we keep His command-ments, and do those things that are pleasing in His sight.
1 John 3:21-22

Praise and Thanksgiving
"O Come, let us sing unto the LORD: let us make a joyful noise to the rock of our salvation . . . O come, let us worship and bow down: let us kneel before the LORD our Maker."
Psalm 95:1, 6

_____

_____

Repent through Confession
'Therefore say thou unto them, Thus saith the LORD of hosts; Turn ye unto Me, saith the LORD of hosts, and I will turn unto you, saith the LORD of hosts."
Zechariah 1:3

"Draw nigh to God, and He will draw nigh unto you. Cleanse your hands, ye sinners; and purify your hearts, ye double minded."
James 4:8

_____

_____

Ask
"And His disciples came to Him, and awoke Him, saying, LORD, save us: we perish. And He saith unto them, Why are ye fearful, O ye of little faith? Then He arose, and rebuked the winds and the sea; and there was great calm."
Matthew 8:26

"Likewise the Spirit also helpeth our infirmities: for we know not what we should pray for as we ought: but the Spirit itself maketh intercession for us with groanings which cannot be uttered."
Romans 8:26

Personal needs: **Date Entered**   **Date Answered**

_____

_____

Personal desires for the glory of God:

_____

_____

(Yield to the Father) Prayer of surrender to the will of the Father
"Submit yourselves therefore to God. Resist the devil, and he will flee
from you." James 4:7

_____

_____

_____

_____

_____

Examine and Reflect
"Let my cry come near before The, O LORD: give me understanding
according to Thy word." Psalm 119:169

_____

_____

_____

_____

_____

_____

_____

Notes

_____

_____

_____

_____

_____

_____

_____

_____

_____

_____

Date_____

"He hears and answers every prayer, where the *true conditions* of praying
are met." (*italics* inserted for emphasis)

E. M. Bounds, "The Possibilities of Prayer"

"And this is the confidence that we have in Him, that, if we ask anything
according to His will, He heareth us: And if we know that He hear us,
whatsoever we ask, we know that we have the petitions that we desired if
Him."   I John 5:14-15

Praise and Thanksgiving

"O Come, let us sing unto the LORD: let us make a joyful noise to the rock
of our salvation . . . O come, let us worship and bow down: let us kneel
before the LORD our Maker."   Psalm 95:1, 6

_____

_____

Repent through Confession

'Therefore say thou unto them, Thus saith the LORD of hosts; Turn ye unto
Me, saith the LORD of hosts, and I will turn unto you, saith the LORD of
hosts."   Zechariah 1:3

"Draw nigh to God, and He will draw nigh unto you. Cleanse your hands,
ye sinners; and purify your hearts, ye double minded."   James 4:8

_____

_____

Ask

"Ask, and it shall be given you; seek, and you shall find; knock, and it
shall be opened unto you: for everyone that asketh receiveth; and he that
seeketh findeth; and to him that knocketh it shall be opened."

Matthew 7:7-8

Salvation

"For by grace are you saved through faith; . . . it is the gift of God"

Ephesians 2:8

Name	Date Entered	Date Answered

Yield to the Father (Prayer of surrender to the will of the Father)

"Nevertheless not what I will, but what thou wilt."   Mark 14:36b

Examine and Reflect

"Examine yourselves, whether ye be in faith; prove your own selves."

2 Corinthians 13:5

Notes

Date_____

"The effectual fervent prayer of a righteous man availeth much."

James 5:16b

Praise and Thanksgiving

"O Come, let us sing unto the LORD: let us make a joyful noise to the rock of our salvation . . . O come, let us worship and bow down: let us kneel before the LORD our Maker." Psalm 95:1, 6

_____

_____

Repent through Confession

'Therefore say thou unto them, Thus saith the LORD of hosts; Turn ye unto Me, saith the LORD of hosts, and I will turn unto you, saith the LORD of hosts." Zechariah 1:3

"Draw nigh to God, and He will draw nigh unto you. Cleanse your hands, ye sinners; and purify your hearts, ye double minded." James 4:8

_____

_____

Ask

"Therefore I say unto you, What things soever ye desire, when ye pray, believe that ye receive them, and ye shall have them" Mark 11:24

Church Leadership

"Finally, brethren, pray for us, that the word of the LORD may have free course, and be glorified, as as it is with you." 2 Thessalonians 3:1

"Behold, how good and how pleasant it is for the brethren to dwell together in unity." Psalm 133:1

Senior Pastor: (Personal) _____
(Professional) _____
Associate Pastor/Administrator: (Personal) _____
(Professional) _____

Associate Pastor/Music: (Personal) _____
(Professional) _____
Associate Pastor/Education: (Personal) _____
(Professional) _____
Children's Ministry Director: (Personal) _____
(Professional) _____
Other Ministerial Staff _____
Other Ministerial Staff _____
Other Ministerial Staff _____

Yield to the Father (Prayer of surrender to the will of the Father)

"Humble yourselves in the sight of the LORD, and He shall lift you up.

James 4:10

_____
_____
_____
_____

Examine and Reflect

"Examine me, O LORD, and prove me: . . ."   Psalm 26:2

_____
_____
_____
_____
_____
_____
_____

Date_____

"Let us therefore come boldly unto the throne of grace, that we may obtain mercy, and find grace to help in time of need.   Hebrews 4:16

Praise and Thanksgiving
"O Come, let us sing unto the LORD: let us make a joyful noise to the rock of our salvation . . . O come, let us worship and bow down: let us kneel before the LORD our Maker."   Psalm 95:1, 6

_____

_____

Repent through Confession
'Therefore say thou unto them, Thus saith the LORD of hosts; Turn ye unto Me, saith the LORD of hosts, and I will turn unto you, saith the LORD of hosts."   Zechariah 1:3

"Draw nigh to God, and He will draw nigh unto you. Cleanse your hands, ye sinners; and purify your hearts, ye double minded."   James 4:8

_____

_____

Ask
"If ye abide in Me, and my words abide in you, ye shall ask what ye will, and it shall be done unto you."   John 15:7

Government Leadership and Policy-makers
"I exhort therefore, that, first of all, supplications, prayers, intercessions, and giving of thanks be made for all men; for kings, and for all that are in authority; that we may lead a quiet and peaceable life in all godliness and honesty."   1 Timothy 2:1-3

National:_____

_____

_____

State:_____

_____

_____

Local_____

_____

_____

Yield to the Father (Prayer of surrender to the will of the Father)

"Obey them that have the rule over you, and submit yourselves: for they watch for your souls, as they that must give account, that they may do it with joy, and not with grief: for that is unprofitable for you."

Hebrews 13:17

_____

_____

_____

_____

_____

Examine and Reflect

"But let every man prove his own work, and then shall he have rejoicing in himself alone, and not in another." Galatians 6:4

_____

_____

_____

_____

_____

_____

Notes

_____

_____

_____

_____

_____

Date_____

"Call unto Me, and I will answer thee, and shew thee great and might things, which thou knowest not.   Jeremiah 33:3

Praise and Thanksgiving
"O Come, let us sing unto the LORD: let us make a joyful noise to the rock of our salvation . . . O come, let us worship and bow down: let us kneel before the LORD our Maker."   Psalm 95:1, 6

_____

_____

Repent through Confession
'Therefore say thou unto them, Thus saith the LORD of hosts; Turn ye unto Me, saith the LORD of hosts, and I will turn unto you, saith the LORD of hosts."   Zechariah 1:3

"Draw nigh to God, and He will draw nigh unto you. Cleanse your hands, ye sinners; and purify your hearts, ye double minded."   James 4:8

_____

_____

Ask
"And all things, whatsoever ye shall ask in prayer, believing, ye shall receive.   Matthew 21:22

Active Military members:

Name	Need	Date Entered	Date Answered

Missionaries

_____

_____

_____

_____

Yield to the Father (Prayer of surrender to the will of the Father)
"Nevertheless not what I will, but what thou wilt." Mark 14:36

_____

_____

_____

_____

_____

Examine and Reflect
"Examine yourselves, whether ye be in the faith; prove your own selves.
Know ye not your own selves, how that Jesus Christ is in your, except ye
be reprobates? 2 Corinthians 13:5

_____

_____

_____

_____

_____

_____

Notes

_____

_____

_____

_____

_____

_____

_____

_____

_____

_____

_____

_____

_____

_____

Date_____

"Now unto Him that is able to do exceeding abundantly above all that we ask or think, according to the power that worketh in us. Ephesians 3:20

Praise and Thanksgiving
"O Come, let us sing unto the LORD: let us make a joyful noise to the rock of our salvation . . . O come, let us worship and bow down: let us kneel before the LORD our Maker." Psalm 95:1, 6

_____

_____

Repent through Confession
'Therefore say thou unto them, Thus saith the LORD of hosts; Turn ye unto Me, saith the LORD of hosts, and I will turn unto you, saith the LORD of hosts." Zechariah 1:3

"Draw nigh to God, and He will draw nigh unto you. Cleanse your hands, ye sinners; and purify your hearts, ye double minded." James 4:8

_____

_____

Ask
"As, and it shall be given you; seek, and you shall find; knock, and it shall be opened unto you: for everyone that asketh receiveth; and he that seeketh findeth; and to him that knocketh it shall be opened." Matthew 7:7-8

Physically ill
"The prayer of faith shall save the sick, and the LORD shall raise him." James 5:15

Name	Need	Date Entered	Date Answered

Yield to the Father (Prayer of surrender to the will of the Father)

"Know ye not, that to whom ye yield yourself servants to obey, his servants ye are to whom ye obey; whether of sin unto death, or of obedience unto righteousness?"

Romans 6:16

_____
_____
_____
_____
_____

Examine and Reflect

"Search me, O God, and know my heart: try me, and know my thoughts. And see if there be any wicked way in me, and lead me in the way everlasting."

Psalm 139:23-24

_____
_____
_____
_____
_____
_____

Notes

_____
_____
_____
_____
_____
_____
_____
_____
_____
_____
_____
_____
_____
_____
_____

Date_____

".. . the will of the LORD be done." Acts 21:14

Praise and Thanksgiving
"O Come, let us sing unto the LORD: let us make a joyful noise to the rock
of our salvation . . . O come, let us worship and bow down: let us kneel
before the LORD our Maker." Psalm 95:1, 6

_____

_____

Repent through Confession
'Therefore say thou unto them, Thus saith the LORD of hosts; Turn ye unto
Me, saith the LORD of hosts, and I will turn unto you, saith the LORD of
hosts." Zechariah 1:3

"Draw nigh to God, and He will draw nigh unto you. Cleanse your hands,
ye sinners; and purify your hearts, ye double minded." James 4:8

_____

_____

Ask
"But my God shall supply all your need according to His riches in glory
by Christ Jesus. Philippians 4:19

Those with Relationship Problems:

Name	Need	Date Entered	Date Answered

Yield to the Father (**Prayer of surrender to the will of the Father**)

"Neither yield ye your members as instruments of unrighteousness unto sin: but yield yourselves unto God, as those that are alive from the dead, and your members as instruments of righteousness unto God."

Romans 6:13

Examine and **R**eflect

"Judge me, O LORD; for I have walked in my integrity; I have trusted also in the LORD; therefore I shall not slide." Psalm 26:1

Notes

Date_____

"Beloved, if our heart condemn us not, then have we confidence toward God. And whatsoever we ask, we receive of Him, because we keep His command-ments, and do those things that are pleasing in His sight.

1 John 3:21-22

Praise and Thanksgiving
"O Come, let us sing unto the LORD: let us make a joyful noise to the rock of our salvation . . . O come, let us worship and bow down: let us kneel before the LORD our Maker."   Psalm 95:1, 6

_____

_____

Repent through Confession
'Therefore say thou unto them, Thus saith the LORD of hosts; Turn ye unto Me, saith the LORD of hosts, and I will turn unto you, saith the LORD of hosts."   Zechariah 1:3

"Draw nigh to God, and He will draw nigh unto you. Cleanse your hands, ye sinners; and purify your hearts, ye double minded."   James 4:8

_____

_____

Ask
"And His disciples came to Him, and awoke Him, saying, LORD, save us: we perish. And He saith unto them, Why are ye fearful, O ye of little faith? Then He arose, and rebuked the winds and the sea; and there was great calm."   Matthew 8:26

"Likewise the Spirit also helpeth our infirmities: for we know not what we should pray for as we ought: but the Spirit itself maketh intercession for us with groanings which cannot be uttered."   Romans 8:26

Personal needs: **Date Entered**   **Date Answered**

_____

_____

Personal desires for the glory of God:

_____

_____

(<u>Y</u>ield to the Father) Prayer of surrender to the will of the Father
"Submit yourselves therefore to God. Resist the devil, and he will flee
from you."   James 4:7

_____

_____

_____

_____

_____

<u>E</u>xamine and <u>R</u>eflect
"Let my cry come near before The, O Lord: give me understanding
according to Thy word."   Psalm 119:169

_____

_____

_____

_____

_____

_____

_____

Notes

_____

_____

_____

_____

_____

_____

_____

_____

_____

_____

_____

Date_____

"He hears and answers every prayer, where the *true conditions* of praying are met." (*italics* inserted for emphasis)

E. M. Bounds, "The Possibilities of Prayer"

"And this is the confidence that we have in Him, that, if we ask anything according to His will, He heareth us: And if we know that He hear us, whatsoever we ask, we know that we have the petitions that we desired if Him."

I John 5:14-15

Praise and Thanksgiving
"O Come, let us sing unto the LORD: let us make a joyful noise to the rock of our salvation . . . O come, let us worship and bow down: let us kneel before the LORD our Maker."

Psalm 95:1, 6

_____

_____

Repent through Confession
'Therefore say thou unto them, Thus saith the LORD of hosts; Turn ye unto Me, saith the LORD of hosts, and I will turn unto you, saith the LORD of hosts."

Zechariah 1:3

"Draw nigh to God, and He will draw nigh unto you. Cleanse your hands, ye sinners; and purify your hearts, ye double minded."

James 4:8

_____

_____

Ask
"Ask, and it shall be given you; seek, and you shall find; knock, and it shall be opened unto you: for everyone that asketh receiveth; and he that seeketh findeth; and to him that knocketh it shall be opened."

Matthew 7:7-8

Salvation

"For by grace are you saved through faith; . . . it is the gift of God"

Ephesians 2:8

Name	Date Entered	Date Answered

(Yield to the Father) Prayer of surrender to the will of the Father

"Submit yourselves therefore to God. Resist the devil, and he will flee from you."

James 4:7

Examine and Reflect

"Let my cry come near before The, O LORD: give me understanding according to Thy word."

Psalm 119:169

Notes

Date_____

"The effectual fervent prayer of a righteous man availeth much."

James 5:16b

Praise and Thanksgiving

"O Come, let us sing unto the LORD: let us make a joyful noise to the rock of our salvation . . . O come, let us worship and bow down: let us kneel before the LORD our Maker." Psalm 95:1, 6

_____

_____

Repent through Confession

'Therefore say thou unto them, Thus saith the LORD of hosts; Turn ye unto Me, saith the LORD of hosts, and I will turn unto you, saith the LORD of hosts." Zechariah 1:3

"Draw nigh to God, and He will draw nigh unto you. Cleanse your hands, ye sinners; and purify your hearts, ye double minded." James 4:8

_____

_____

Ask

"Therefore I say unto you, What things soever ye desire, when ye pray, believe that ye receive them, and ye shall have them" Mark 11:24

Church Leadership

"Finally, brethren, pray for us, that the word of the LORD may have free course, and be glorified, as as it is with you." 2 Thessalonians 3:1

"Behold, how good and how pleasant it is for the brethren to dwell together in unity." Psalm 133:1

Senior Pastor: (Personal) _____
(Professional) _____
Associate Pastor/Administrator: (Personal) _____
(Professional) _____

Associate Pastor/Music: (Personal) _____
(Professional) _____
Associate Pastor/Education: (Personal) _____
(Professional) _____
Children's Ministry Director: (Personal) _____
(Professional) _____
Other Ministerial Staff _____
Other Ministerial Staff _____
Other Ministerial Staff _____

Y̲ield to the Father (Prayer of surrender to the will of the Father)
"Humble yourselves in the sight of the LORD, and He shall lift you up.

James 4:10

_____
_____
_____
_____

E̲xamine and R̲eflect
"Examine me, O LORD, and prove me: . . ."   Psalm 26:2

_____
_____
_____
_____
_____
_____
_____

Date_____

"Let us therefore come boldly unto the throne of grace, that we may obtain mercy, and find grace to help in time of need.   Hebrews 4:16

Praise and Thanksgiving
"O Come, let us sing unto the LORD: let us make a joyful noise to the rock of our salvation . . . O come, let us worship and bow down: let us kneel before the LORD our Maker."   Psalm 95:1, 6

_____

_____

Repent through Confession
'Therefore say thou unto them, Thus saith the LORD of hosts; Turn ye unto Me, saith the LORD of hosts, and I will turn unto you, saith the LORD of hosts."   Zechariah 1:3

"Draw nigh to God, and He will draw nigh unto you. Cleanse your hands, ye sinners; and purify your hearts, ye double minded."   James 4:8

_____

_____

Ask
"If ye abide in Me, and my words abide in you, ye shall ask what ye will, and it shall be done unto you."   John 15:7

Government Leadership and Policy-makers
"I exhort therefore, that, first of all, supplications, prayers, intercessions, and giving of thanks be made for all men; for kings, and for all that are in authority; that we may lead a quiet and peaceable life in all godliness and honesty."   1 Timothy 2:1-3

National:_____

_____

_____

State:_____
_____
_____

Local_____
_____
_____

Yield to the Father (Prayer of surrender to the will of the Father)

"Obey them that have the rule over you, and submit yourselves: for they watch for your souls, as they that must give account, that they may do it with joy, and not with grief: for that is unprofitable for you."

Hebrews 13:17

_____
_____
_____
_____
_____

Examine and **R**eflect

"But let every man prove his own work, and then shall he have rejoicing in himself alone, and not in another." Galatians 6:4

_____
_____
_____
_____
_____
_____

Notes

_____
_____
_____
_____
_____

Date_____

"Call unto Me, and I will answer thee, and shew thee great and might things, which thou knowest not.   Jeremiah 33:3

Praise and Thanksgiving

"O Come, let us sing unto the LORD: let us make a joyful noise to the rock of our salvation . . . O come, let us worship and bow down: let us kneel before the LORD our Maker."   Psalm 95:1, 6

_____

_____

Repent through Confession

'Therefore say thou unto them, Thus saith the LORD of hosts; Turn ye unto Me, saith the LORD of hosts, and I will turn unto you, saith the LORD of hosts."   Zechariah 1:3

"Draw nigh to God, and He will draw nigh unto you. Cleanse your hands, ye sinners; and purify your hearts, ye double minded."   James 4:8

_____

_____

Ask

"And all things, whatsoever ye shall ask in prayer, believing, ye shall receive.   Matthew 21:22

Active Military members:

Name	Need	Date Entered	Date Answered

Missionaries

_____

_____

_____

_____

<u>Y</u>ield to the Father (Prayer of surrender to the will of the Father)

"Nevertheless not what I will, but what thou wilt."　　　　Mark 14:36

_____

_____

_____

_____

_____

<u>E</u>xamine and <u>R</u>eflect

"Examine yourselves, whether ye be in the faith; prove your own selves.
Know ye not your own selves, how that Jesus Christ is in your, except ye
be reprobates?　　　　　　　　　　　　　　2 Corinthians 13:5

_____

_____

_____

_____

_____

_____

Notes

_____

_____

_____

_____

_____

_____

_____

_____

_____

_____

_____

_____

_____

_____

_____

_____

Date_____

"Now unto Him that is able to do exceeding abundantly above all that we ask or think, according to the power that worketh in us. Ephesians 3:20

Praise and Thanksgiving
"O Come, let us sing unto the Lord: let us make a joyful noise to the rock of our salvation . . . O come, let us worship and bow down: let us kneel before the Lord our Maker."   Psalm 95:1, 6

_____

_____

Repent through Confession
'Therefore say thou unto them, Thus saith the Lord of hosts; Turn ye unto Me, saith the Lord of hosts, and I will turn unto you, saith the Lord of hosts."   Zechariah 1:3

"Draw nigh to God, and He will draw nigh unto you. Cleanse your hands, ye sinners; and purify your hearts, ye double minded."   James 4:8

_____

_____

Ask
"As, and it shall be given you; seek, and you shall find; knock, and it shall be opened unto you: for everyone that asketh receiveth; and he that seeketh findeth; and to him that knocketh it shall be opened."
                                                        Matthew 7:7-8

Physically ill
"The prayer of faith shall save the sick, and the Lord shall raise him."
                                                            James 5:15

Name	Need	Date Entered	Date Answered

Yield to the Father (Prayer of surrender to the will of the Father)

"Know ye not, that to whom ye yield yourself servants to obey, his servants ye are to whom ye obey; whether of sin unto death, or of obedience unto righteousness?"

Romans 6:16

_____

_____

_____

_____

_____

Examine and Reflect

"Search me, O God, and know my heart: try me, and know my thoughts. And see if there be any wicked way in me, and lead me in the way everlasting."

Psalm 139:23-24

_____

_____

_____

_____

_____

Notes

_____

_____

_____

_____

_____

_____

_____

_____

_____

_____

_____

_____

Date_____

".. . the will of the Lord be done." Acts 21:14

Praise and Thanksgiving
"O Come, let us sing unto the Lord: let us make a joyful noise to the rock
of our salvation . . . O come, let us worship and bow down: let us kneel
before the Lord our Maker." Psalm 95:1, 6

_____

_____

Repent through Confession
'Therefore say thou unto them, Thus saith the Lord of hosts; Turn ye unto
Me, saith the Lord of hosts, and I will turn unto you, saith the Lord of
hosts." Zechariah 1:3

"Draw nigh to God, and He will draw nigh unto you. Cleanse your hands,
ye sinners; and purify your hearts, ye double minded." James 4:8

_____

_____

Ask
"But my God shall supply all your need according to His riches in glory
by Christ Jesus. Philippians 4:19

Those with Relationship Problems:

Name	Need	Date Entered	Date Answered

Yield to the Father (Prayer of surrender to the will of the Father)
"Neither yield ye your members as instruments of unrighteousness unto sin: but yield yourselves unto God, as those that are alive from the dead, and your members as instruments of righteousness unto God."

Romans 6:13

_____
_____
_____
_____

Examine and Reflect
"Judge me, O LORD; for I have walked in my integrity; I have trusted also in the LORD; therefore I shall not slide."

Psalm 26:1

_____
_____
_____
_____
_____
_____

Notes

_____
_____
_____
_____
_____
_____
_____
_____
_____
_____
_____
_____
_____
_____
_____

Date_____

"Beloved, if our heart condemn us not, then have we confidence toward God. And whatsoever we ask, we receive of Him, because we keep His command-ments, and do those things that are pleasing in His sight.
1 John 3:21-22

Praise and Thanksgiving
"O Come, let us sing unto the LORD: let us make a joyful noise to the rock of our salvation . . . O come, let us worship and bow down: let us kneel before the LORD our Maker."   Psalm 95:1, 6

_____

_____

Repent through Confession
'Therefore say thou unto them, Thus saith the LORD of hosts; Turn ye unto Me, saith the LORD of hosts, and I will turn unto you, saith the LORD of hosts."   Zechariah 1:3

"Draw nigh to God, and He will draw nigh unto you. Cleanse your hands, ye sinners; and purify your hearts, ye double minded."   James 4:8

_____

_____

Ask
"And His disciples came to Him, and awoke Him, saying, LORD, save us: we perish. And He saith unto them, Why are ye fearful, O ye of little faith? Then He arose, and rebuked the winds and the sea; and there was great calm."   Matthew 8:26

"Likewise the Spirit also helpeth our infirmities: for we know not what we should pray for as we ought: but the Spirit itself maketh intercession for us with groanings which cannot be uttered."   Romans 8:26

Personal needs: **Date Entered**   **Date Answered**

_____

_____

Personal desires for the glory of God:

_____

_____

Yield to the Father (Prayer of surrender to the will of the Father)
"Neither yield ye your members as instruments of unrighteousness unto
sin: but yield yourselves unto God, as those that are alive from the dead,
and your members as instruments of righteousness unto God."

Romans 6:13

_____

_____

_____

_____

Examine and **R**eflect
"Judge me, O LORD; for I have walked in my integrity; I have trusted also
in the LORD; therefore I shall not slide."   Psalm 26:1

_____

_____

_____

_____

_____

_____

Notes

_____

_____

_____

_____

_____

_____

_____

_____

_____

_____

_____

Date_____

"He hears and answers every prayer, where the *true conditions* of praying are met." (*italics* inserted for emphasis)

E. M. Bounds, "The Possibilities of Prayer"

"And this is the confidence that we have in Him, that, if we ask anything according to His will, He heareth us: And if we know that He hear us, whatsoever we ask, we know that we have the petitions that we desired if Him."

I John 5:14-15

Praise and Thanksgiving

"O Come, let us sing unto the LORD: let us make a joyful noise to the rock of our salvation . . . O come, let us worship and bow down: let us kneel before the LORD our Maker."

Psalm 95:1, 6

_____

_____

Repent through Confession

'Therefore say thou unto them, Thus saith the LORD of hosts; Turn ye unto Me, saith the LORD of hosts, and I will turn unto you, saith the LORD of hosts."

Zechariah 1:3

"Draw nigh to God, and He will draw nigh unto you. Cleanse your hands, ye sinners; and purify your hearts, ye double minded."

James 4:8

_____

_____

Ask

"Ask, and it shall be given you; seek, and you shall find; knock, and it shall be opened unto you: for everyone that asketh receiveth; and he that seeketh findeth; and to him that knocketh it shall be opened."

Matthew 7:7-8

Salvation

"For by grace are you saved through faith; . . . it is the gift of God"

Ephesians 2:8

Name	Date Entered	Date Answered

Yield to the Father (Prayer of surrender to the will of the Father)

"Nevertheless not what I will, but what thou wilt."   Mark 14:36b

_____

_____

_____

_____

Examine and **R**eflect

"Examine yourselves, whether ye be in faith; prove your own selves."

2 Corinthians 13:5

_____

_____

_____

_____

_____

_____

Notes

_____

_____

_____

_____

_____

_____

_____

_____

Date_____

"The effectual fervent prayer of a righteous man availeth much."

James 5:16b

Praise and Thanksgiving
"O Come, let us sing unto the LORD: let us make a joyful noise to the rock of our salvation . . . O come, let us worship and bow down: let us kneel before the LORD our Maker."   Psalm 95:1, 6

_____

_____

Repent through Confession
'Therefore say thou unto them, Thus saith the LORD of hosts; Turn ye unto Me, saith the LORD of hosts, and I will turn unto you, saith the LORD of hosts."   Zechariah 1:3

"Draw nigh to God, and He will draw nigh unto you. Cleanse your hands, ye sinners; and purify your hearts, ye double minded."   James 4:8

_____

_____

Ask
"Therefore I say unto you, What things soever ye desire, when ye pray, believe that ye receive them, and ye shall have them"   Mark 11:24

Church Leadership
"Finally, brethren, pray for us, that the word of the LORD may have free course, and be glorified, as as it is with you."   2 Thessalonians 3:1

"Behold, how good and how pleasant it is for the brethren to dwell together in unity."   Psalm 133:1

Senior Pastor: (Personal) _____
(Professional) _____
Associate Pastor/Administrator: (Personal) _____
(Professional) _____

Associate Pastor/Music: (Personal) _____

(Professional) _____

Associate Pastor/Education: (Personal) _____

(Professional) _____

Children's Ministry Director: (Personal) _____

(Professional) _____

Other Ministerial Staff _____

Other Ministerial Staff _____

Other Ministerial Staff _____

Yield **to the Father (Prayer of surrender to the will of the Father)**

"Humble yourselves in the sight of the LORD, and He shall lift you up.

James 4:10

_____

_____

_____

_____

Examine **and R**eflect

"Examine me, O LORD, and prove me: . . ."   Psalm 26:2

_____

_____

_____

_____

_____

_____

_____

Date_____

"Let us therefore come boldly unto the throne of grace, that we may obtain mercy, and find grace to help in time of need.   Hebrews 4:16

Praise and Thanksgiving

"O Come, let us sing unto the LORD: let us make a joyful noise to the rock of our salvation . . . O come, let us worship and bow down: let us kneel before the LORD our Maker."   Psalm 95:1, 6

_____

_____

Repent through Confession

'Therefore say thou unto them, Thus saith the LORD of hosts; Turn ye unto Me, saith the LORD of hosts, and I will turn unto you, saith the LORD of hosts."   Zechariah 1:3

"Draw nigh to God, and He will draw nigh unto you. Cleanse your hands, ye sinners; and purify your hearts, ye double minded."   James 4:8

_____

_____

Ask

"If ye abide in Me, and my words abide in you, ye shall ask what ye will, and it shall be done unto you."   John 15:7

Government Leadership and Policy-makers

"I exhort therefore, that, first of all, supplications, prayers, intercessions, and giving of thanks be made for all men; for kings, and for all that are in authority; that we may lead a quiet and peaceable life in all godliness and honesty."   1 Timothy 2:1-3

National:_____

_____

_____

State:_____

_____

_____

Local_____

_____

_____

Yield to the Father (Prayer of surrender to the will of the Father)
"Obey them that have the rule over you, and submit yourselves: for they watch for your souls, as they that must give account, that they may do it with joy, and not with grief: for that is unprofitable for you."

Hebrews 13:17

_____

_____

_____

_____

_____

Examine and Reflect
"But let every man prove his own work, and then shall he have rejoicing in himself alone, and not in another." Galatians 6:4

_____

_____

_____

_____

_____

_____

Notes

_____

_____

_____

_____

_____

Date_____

"Call unto Me, and I will answer thee, and shew thee great and might things, which thou knowest not.   Jeremiah 33:3

Praise and Thanksgiving
"O Come, let us sing unto the LORD: let us make a joyful noise to the rock of our salvation . . . O come, let us worship and bow down: let us kneel before the LORD our Maker."   Psalm 95:1, 6

_____

_____

Repent through Confession
'Therefore say thou unto them, Thus saith the LORD of hosts; Turn ye unto Me, saith the LORD of hosts, and I will turn unto you, saith the LORD of hosts."   Zechariah 1:3

"Draw nigh to God, and He will draw nigh unto you. Cleanse your hands, ye sinners; and purify your hearts, ye double minded."   James 4:8

_____

_____

Ask
"And all things, whatsoever ye shall ask in prayer, believing, ye shall receive.   Matthew 21:22

Active Military members:

Name	Need	Date Entered	Date Answered

Missionaries

_____

_____

_____

_____

Yield to the Father (Prayer of surrender to the will of the Father)
"Nevertheless not what I will, but what thou wilt."   Mark 14:36

_____

_____

_____

_____

_____

Examine and Reflect
"Examine yourselves, whether ye be in the faith; prove your own selves.
Know ye not your own selves, how that Jesus Christ is in your, except ye
be reprobates?   2 Corinthians 13:5

_____

_____

_____

_____

_____

Notes

_____

_____

_____

_____

_____

_____

_____

_____

_____

_____

_____

_____

_____

Date_____

"Now unto Him that is able to do exceeding abundantly above all that we ask or think, according to the power that worketh in us. Ephesians 3:20

Praise and Thanksgiving

"O Come, let us sing unto the LORD: let us make a joyful noise to the rock of our salvation . . . O come, let us worship and bow down: let us kneel before the LORD our Maker."   Psalm 95:1, 6

_____

_____

Repent through Confession

'Therefore say thou unto them, Thus saith the LORD of hosts; Turn ye unto Me, saith the LORD of hosts, and I will turn unto you, saith the LORD of hosts."   Zechariah 1:3

"Draw nigh to God, and He will draw nigh unto you. Cleanse your hands, ye sinners; and purify your hearts, ye double minded."   James 4:8

_____

_____

Ask

"As, and it shall be given you; seek, and you shall find; knock, and it shall be opened unto you: for everyone that asketh receiveth; and he that seeketh findeth; and to him that knocketh it shall be opened."

Matthew 7:7-8

Physically ill

"The prayer of faith shall save the sick, and the LORD shall raise him."

James 5:15

Name	Need	Date Entered	Date Answered

<u>Y</u>ield to the Father (Prayer of surrender to the will of the Father)

"Know ye not, that to whom ye yield yourself servants to obey, his servants ye are to whom ye obey; whether of sin unto death, or of obedience unto righteousness?"   Romans 6:16

_____

_____

_____

_____

_____

<u>E</u>xamine and <u>R</u>eflect

"Search me, O God, and know my heart: try me, and know my thoughts. And see if there be any wicked way in me, and lead me in the way everlasting."   Psalm 139:23-24

_____

_____

_____

_____

_____

Notes

_____

_____

_____

_____

_____

_____

_____

_____

_____

_____

_____

_____

_____

Date_____

". . . the will of the LORD be done."   Acts 21:14

Praise and Thanksgiving
"O Come, let us sing unto the LORD: let us make a joyful noise to the rock of our salvation . . . O come, let us worship and bow down: let us kneel before the LORD our Maker."   Psalm 95:1, 6

_____

_____

Repent through Confession
'Therefore say thou unto them, Thus saith the LORD of hosts; Turn ye unto Me, saith the LORD of hosts, and I will turn unto you, saith the LORD of hosts."   Zechariah 1:3

"Draw nigh to God, and He will draw nigh unto you. Cleanse your hands, ye sinners; and purify your hearts, ye double minded."   James 4:8

_____

_____

Ask
"But my God shall supply all your need according to His riches in glory by Christ Jesus.   Philippians 4:19

Those with Relationship Problems:

Name	Need	Date Entered	Date Answered

<u>Y</u>ield to the Father (Prayer of surrender to the will of the Father)

"Neither yield ye your members as instruments of unrighteousness unto sin: but yield yourselves unto God, as those that are alive from the dead, and your members as instruments of righteousness unto God."

Romans 6:13

_____
_____
_____
_____

<u>E</u>xamine and <u>R</u>eflect

"Judge me, O Lord; for I have walked in my integrity; I have trusted also in the Lord; therefore I shall not slide."

Psalm 26:1

_____
_____
_____
_____
_____
_____

Notes

_____
_____
_____
_____
_____
_____
_____
_____
_____
_____
_____
_____
_____
_____

Date_____

"Beloved, if our heart condemn us not, then have we confidence toward God. And whatsoever we ask, we receive of Him, because we keep His commandments, and do those things that are pleasing in His sight.
1 John 3:21-22

Praise and Thanksgiving

"O Come, let us sing unto the LORD: let us make a joyful noise to the rock of our salvation . . . O come, let us worship and bow down: let us kneel before the LORD our Maker."
Psalm 95:1, 6

_____

_____

Repent through Confession

'Therefore say thou unto them, Thus saith the LORD of hosts; Turn ye unto Me, saith the LORD of hosts, and I will turn unto you, saith the LORD of hosts."
Zechariah 1:3

"Draw nigh to God, and He will draw nigh unto you. Cleanse your hands, ye sinners; and purify your hearts, ye double minded."
James 4:8

_____

_____

Ask

"And His disciples came to Him, and awoke Him, saying, LORD, save us: we perish. And He saith unto them, Why are ye fearful, O ye of little faith? Then He arose, and rebuked the winds and the sea; and there was great calm."
Matthew 8:26

"Likewise the Spirit also helpeth our infirmities: for we know not what we should pray for as we ought: but the Spirit itself maketh intercession for us with groanings which cannot be uttered."
Romans 8:26

Personal needs: **Date Entered**   **Date Answered**

_____

_____

Personal desires for the glory of God:

_____

_____

(Yield to the Father) Prayer of surrender to the will of the Father
"Submit yourselves therefore to God. Resist the devil, and he will flee
from you."   James 4:7

_____

_____

_____

_____

_____

Examine and Reflect
"Let my cry come near before The, O Lord: give me understanding
according to Thy word."   Psalm 119:169

_____

_____

_____

_____

_____

_____

Notes

_____

_____

_____

_____

_____

_____

_____

_____

_____

_____

Date_____

"He hears and answers every prayer, where the *true conditions* of praying are met." (*italics* inserted for emphasis)

E. M. Bounds, "The Possibilities of Prayer"

"And this is the confidence that we have in Him, that, if we ask anything according to His will, He heareth us: And if we know that He hear us, whatsoever we ask, we know that we have the petitions that we desired if Him." I John 5:14-15

Praise and Thanksgiving
"O Come, let us sing unto the LORD: let us make a joyful noise to the rock of our salvation . . . O come, let us worship and bow down: let us kneel before the LORD our Maker." Psalm 95:1, 6

_____

_____

Repent through Confession
'Therefore say thou unto them, Thus saith the LORD of hosts; Turn ye unto Me, saith the LORD of hosts, and I will turn unto you, saith the LORD of hosts." Zechariah 1:3

"Draw nigh to God, and He will draw nigh unto you. Cleanse your hands, ye sinners; and purify your hearts, ye double minded." James 4:8

_____

_____

Ask
"Ask, and it shall be given you; seek, and you shall find; knock, and it shall be opened unto you: for everyone that asketh receiveth; and he that seeketh findeth; and to him that knocketh it shall be opened." Matthew 7:7-8

Salvation

"For by grace are you saved through faith; . . . it is the gift of God"

Ephesians 2:8

Name	Date Entered	Date Answered

Yield to the Father (Prayer of surrender to the will of the Father)

"Nevertheless not what I will, but what thou wilt."   Mark 14:36b

_____

_____

_____

_____

Examine and Reflect

"Examine yourselves, whether ye be in faith; prove your own selves."

2 Corinthians 13:5

_____

_____

_____

_____

_____

_____

Notes

_____

_____

_____

_____

_____

_____

_____

_____

_____

Date_____

"The effectual fervent prayer of a righteous man availeth much."

James 5:16b

Praise and Thanksgiving

"O Come, let us sing unto the LORD: let us make a joyful noise to the rock of our salvation . . . O come, let us worship and bow down: let us kneel before the LORD our Maker."   Psalm 95:1, 6

_____

_____

Repent through Confession

'Therefore say thou unto them, Thus saith the LORD of hosts; Turn ye unto Me, saith the LORD of hosts, and I will turn unto you, saith the LORD of hosts."   Zechariah 1:3

"Draw nigh to God, and He will draw nigh unto you. Cleanse your hands, ye sinners; and purify your hearts, ye double minded."   James 4:8

_____

_____

Ask

"Therefore I say unto you, What things soever ye desire, when ye pray, believe that ye receive them, and ye shall have them"   Mark 11:24

Church Leadership

"Finally, brethren, pray for us, that the word of the LORD may have free course, and be glorified, as as it is with you."   2 Thessalonians 3:1

"Behold, how good and how pleasant it is for the brethren to dwell together in unity."   Psalm 133:1

Senior Pastor: (Personal) _____

(Professional) _____

Associate Pastor/Administrator: (Personal) _____

(Professional) _____

Associate Pastor/Music: (Personal) _____
(Professional) _____
Associate Pastor/Education: (Personal) _____
(Professional) _____
Children's Ministry Director: (Personal) _____
(Professional) _____
Other Ministerial Staff _____
Other Ministerial Staff _____
Other Ministerial Staff _____

<u>Y</u>ield to the Father (Prayer of surrender to the will of the Father)

"Humble yourselves in the sight of the LORD, and He shall lift you up.

James 4:10

_____
_____
_____
_____

<u>E</u>xamine and <u>R</u>eflect

"Examine me, O LORD, and prove me: . . ."   Psalm 26:2

_____
_____
_____
_____
_____
_____
_____

Date_____

"Let us therefore come boldly unto the throne of grace, that we may obtain mercy, and find grace to help in time of need.   Hebrews 4:16

Praise and Thanksgiving

"O Come, let us sing unto the LORD: let us make a joyful noise to the rock of our salvation . . . O come, let us worship and bow down: let us kneel before the LORD our Maker."   Psalm 95:1, 6

_____

_____

Repent through Confession

'Therefore say thou unto them, Thus saith the LORD of hosts; Turn ye unto Me, saith the LORD of hosts, and I will turn unto you, saith the LORD of hosts."   Zechariah 1:3

"Draw nigh to God, and He will draw nigh unto you. Cleanse your hands, ye sinners; and purify your hearts, ye double minded."   James 4:8

_____

_____

Ask

"If ye abide in Me, and my words abide in you, ye shall ask what ye will, and it shall be done unto you."   John 15:7

Government Leadership and Policy-makers

"I exhort therefore, that, first of all, supplications, prayers, intercessions, and giving of thanks be made for all men; for kings, and for all that are in authority; that we may lead a quiet and peaceable life in all godliness and honesty."   1 Timothy 2:1-3

National:_____

_____

_____

State:_____

_____

_____

Local_____

_____

_____

Yield to the Father (Prayer of surrender to the will of the Father)

"Obey them that have the rule over you, and submit yourselves: for they watch for your souls, as they that must give account, that they may do it with joy, and not with grief: for that is unprofitable for you."

Hebrews 13:17

_____

_____

_____

_____

_____

Examine and **R**eflect

"But let every man prove his own work, and then shall he have rejoicing in himself alone, and not in another." Galatians 6:4

_____

_____

_____

_____

_____

_____

Notes

_____

_____

_____

_____

_____

Date_____

"Call unto Me, and I will answer thee, and shew thee great and might things, which thou knowest not.   Jeremiah 33:3

Praise and Thanksgiving

"I will praise Thee with my whole heart: before the gods will I sing praise unto Thee. I will worship toward Thy holy temple, and praise Thy name for Thy lovingkindness and for Thy truth: for Thou hast magnified Thy word above all Thy name.   Psalm 138: 1-2

Repentance through Confession

"Create in me a clean heart, O, God; and renew a right spirit within me . . . . Restore unto me the joy of Thy salvation.   Psalm 51:10, 12

Ask

"And all things, whatsoever ye shall ask in prayer, believing, ye shall receive.

Matthew 21:22

Active Military members:

Name	Need	Date Entered	Date Answered

Missionaries

_____

_____

_____

_____

_____

_____

_____

_____

Yield to the Father (Prayer of surrender to the will of the Father)
"Nevertheless not what I will, but what thou wilt." Mark 14:36

_____

_____

_____

_____

_____

Examine and Reflect
"Examine yourselves, whether ye be in the faith; prove your own selves.
Know ye not your own selves, how that Jesus Christ is in your, except ye
be reprobates? 2 Corinthians 13:5

_____

_____

_____

_____

_____

Notes

_____

_____

_____

_____

_____

_____

_____

_____

_____

_____

_____

_____

_____

_____

Date_____

"Now unto Him that is able to do exceeding abundantly above all that we ask or think, according to the power that worketh in us. Ephesians 3:20

Praise and Thanksgiving
"O Come, let us sing unto the LORD: let us make a joyful noise to the rock of our salvation . . . O come, let us worship and bow down: let us kneel before the LORD our Maker."   Psalm 95:1, 6

_____

_____

Repent through Confession
'Therefore say thou unto them, Thus saith the LORD of hosts; Turn ye unto Me, saith the LORD of hosts, and I will turn unto you, saith the LORD of hosts."   Zechariah 1:3

"Draw nigh to God, and He will draw nigh unto you. Cleanse your hands, ye sinners; and purify your hearts, ye double minded."   James 4:8

_____

_____

Ask
"As, and it shall be given you; seek, and you shall find; knock, and it shall be opened unto you: for everyone that asketh receiveth; and he that seeketh findeth; and to him that knocketh it shall be opened."
                                                         Matthew 7:7-8

Physically ill
"The prayer of faith shall save the sick, and the LORD shall raise him."
                                                         James 5:15

Name	Need	Date Entered	Date Answered

Yield to the Father (Prayer of surrender to the will of the Father)

"Know ye not, that to whom ye yield yourself servants to obey, his servants ye are to whom ye obey; whether of sin unto death, or of obedience unto righteousness?"

Romans 6:16

_____

_____

_____

_____

_____

Examine and Reflect

"Search me, O God, and know my heart: try me, and know my thoughts. And see if there be any wicked way in me, and lead me in the way everlasting."

Psalm 139:23-24

_____

_____

_____

_____

_____

_____

Notes

_____

_____

_____

_____

_____

_____

_____

_____

_____

_____

_____

_____

Date_____

". . . the will of the LORD be done."   Acts 21:14

Praise and Thanksgiving
"O Come, let us sing unto the LORD: let us make a joyful noise to the rock
of our salvation . . . O come, let us worship and bow down: let us kneel
before the LORD our Maker."   Psalm 95:1, 6

_____

_____

Repent through Confession
'Therefore say thou unto them, Thus saith the LORD of hosts; Turn ye unto
Me, saith the LORD of hosts, and I will turn unto you, saith the LORD of
hosts."   Zechariah 1:3

"Draw nigh to God, and He will draw nigh unto you. Cleanse your hands,
ye sinners; and purify your hearts, ye double minded."   James 4:8

_____

_____

Ask
"But my God shall supply all your need according to His riches in glory
by Christ Jesus.   Philippians 4:19

Those with Relationship Problems:

Name	Need	Date Entered	Date Answered

<u>Y</u>ield to the Father (Prayer of surrender to the will of the Father)

"Neither yield ye your members as instruments of unrighteousness unto sin: but yield yourselves unto God, as those that are alive from the dead, and your members as instruments of righteousness unto God."

Romans 6:13

_____

_____

_____

_____

<u>E</u>xamine and <u>R</u>eflect

"Judge me, O LORD; for I have walked in my integrity; I have trusted also in the LORD; therefore I shall not slide."   Psalm 26:1

_____

_____

_____

_____

_____

_____

Notes

_____

_____

_____

_____

_____

_____

_____

_____

_____

_____

_____

_____

_____

Date_____

"Beloved, if our heart condemn us not, then have we confidence toward God. And whatsoever we ask, we receive of Him, because we keep His command-ments, and do those things that are pleasing in His sight.

1 John 3:21-22

Praise and Thanksgiving
"O Come, let us sing unto the LORD: let us make a joyful noise to the rock of our salvation . . . O come, let us worship and bow down: let us kneel before the LORD our Maker." Psalm 95:1, 6

_____

_____

Repent through Confession
'Therefore say thou unto them, Thus saith the LORD of hosts; Turn ye unto Me, saith the LORD of hosts, and I will turn unto you, saith the LORD of hosts." Zechariah 1:3

"Draw nigh to God, and He will draw nigh unto you. Cleanse your hands, ye sinners; and purify your hearts, ye double minded." James 4:8

_____

_____

Ask
"And His disciples came to Him, and awoke Him, saying, LORD, save us: we perish. And He saith unto them, Why are ye fearful, O ye of little faith? Then He arose, and rebuked the winds and the sea; and there was great calm." Matthew 8:26

"Likewise the Spirit also helpeth our infirmities: for we know not what we should pray for as we ought: but the Spirit itself maketh intercession for us with groanings which cannot be uttered." Romans 8:26

Personal needs: **Date Entered**   **Date Answered**

_____

_____

Personal desires for the glory of God:

_____

_____

(Yield to the Father) Prayer of surrender to the will of the Father

"Submit yourselves therefore to God. Resist the devil, and he will flee from you."   James 4:7

_____

_____

_____

_____

_____

Examine and Reflect

"Let my cry come near before The, O LORD: give me understanding according to Thy word."   Psalm 119:169

_____

_____

_____

_____

_____

_____

Notes

_____

_____

_____

_____

_____

_____

_____

_____

_____

_____

_____

Date_____

"He hears and answers every prayer, where the *true conditions* of praying are met." (*italics* inserted for emphasis)

E. M. Bounds, "The Possibilities of Prayer"

"And this is the confidence that we have in Him, that, if we ask anything according to His will, He heareth us: And if we know that He hear us, whatsoever we ask, we know that we have the petitions that we desired if Him."

I John 5:14-15

Praise and Thanksgiving

"O Come, let us sing unto the LORD: let us make a joyful noise to the rock of our salvation . . . O come, let us worship and bow down: let us kneel before the LORD our Maker."

Psalm 95:1, 6

_____

_____

Repent through Confession

'Therefore say thou unto them, Thus saith the LORD of hosts; Turn ye unto Me, saith the LORD of hosts, and I will turn unto you, saith the LORD of hosts."

Zechariah 1:3

"Draw nigh to God, and He will draw nigh unto you. Cleanse your hands, ye sinners; and purify your hearts, ye double minded."

James 4:8

_____

_____

Ask

"Ask, and it shall be given you; seek, and you shall find; knock, and it shall be opened unto you: for everyone that asketh receiveth; and he that seeketh findeth; and to him that knocketh it shall be opened."

Matthew 7:7-8

Salvation

"For by grace are you saved through faith; . . . it is the gift of God"

Ephesians 2:8

Name	Date Entered	Date Answered

Yield to the Father (Prayer of surrender to the will of the Father)

"Nevertheless not what I will, but what thou wilt."   Mark 14:36b

_____

_____

_____

_____

Examine and Reflect

"Examine yourselves, whether ye be in faith; prove your own selves."

2 Corinthians 13:5

_____

_____

_____

_____

_____

_____

Notes

_____

_____

_____

_____

_____

_____

_____

_____

_____

Date_____

"The effectual fervent prayer of a righteous man availeth much."

James 5:16b

Praise and Thanksgiving

"O Come, let us sing unto the LORD: let us make a joyful noise to the rock of our salvation . . . O come, let us worship and bow down: let us kneel before the LORD our Maker." Psalm 95:1, 6

_____

_____

Repent through Confession

'Therefore say thou unto them, Thus saith the LORD of hosts; Turn ye unto Me, saith the LORD of hosts, and I will turn unto you, saith the LORD of hosts." Zechariah 1:3

"Draw nigh to God, and He will draw nigh unto you. Cleanse your hands, ye sinners; and purify your hearts, ye double minded." James 4:8

_____

_____

Ask

"Therefore I say unto you, What things soever ye desire, when ye pray, believe that ye receive them, and ye shall have them" Mark 11:24

Church Leadership

"Finally, brethren, pray for us, that the word of the LORD may have free course, and be glorified, as as it is with you." 2 Thessalonians 3:1

"Behold, how good and how pleasant it is for the brethren to dwell together in unity." Psalm 133:1

Senior Pastor: (Personal) _____
(Professional) _____
Associate Pastor/Administrator: (Personal) _____
(Professional) _____

Associate Pastor/Music: (Personal) _____

(Professional) _____

Associate Pastor/Education: (Personal) _____

(Professional) _____

Children's Ministry Director: (Personal) _____

(Professional) _____

Other Ministerial Staff _____

Other Ministerial Staff _____

Other Ministerial Staff _____

Yield to the Father (Prayer of surrender to the will of the Father)

"Humble yourselves in the sight of the LORD, and He shall lift you up.

James 4:10

_____

_____

_____

_____

Examine and Reflect

"Examine me, O LORD, and prove me: . . ."   Psalm 26:2

_____

_____

_____

_____

_____

_____

_____

Date_____

"Let us therefore come boldly unto the throne of grace, that we may obtain mercy, and find grace to help in time of need.   Hebrews 4:16

Praise and Thanksgiving
"O Come, let us sing unto the LORD: let us make a joyful noise to the rock of our salvation . . . O come, let us worship and bow down: let us kneel before the LORD our Maker."   Psalm 95:1, 6

_____

_____

Repent through Confession
'Therefore say thou unto them, Thus saith the LORD of hosts; Turn ye unto Me, saith the LORD of hosts, and I will turn unto you, saith the LORD of hosts."   Zechariah 1:3

"Draw nigh to God, and He will draw nigh unto you. Cleanse your hands, ye sinners; and purify your hearts, ye double minded."   James 4:8

_____

_____

Ask
"If ye abide in Me, and my words abide in you, ye shall ask what ye will, and it shall be done unto you."   John 15:7

Government Leadership and Policy-makers
"I exhort therefore, that, first of all, supplications, prayers, intercessions, and giving of thanks be made for all men; for kings, and for all that are in authority; that we may lead a quiet and peaceable life in all godliness and honesty."   1 Timothy 2:1-3

National:_____

_____

_____

State:_____

_____

_____

Local_____

_____

_____

Y̲ield to the Father (Prayer of surrender to the will of the Father)
"Obey them that have the rule over you, and submit yourselves: for they watch for your souls, as they that must give account, that they may do it with joy, and not with grief: for that is unprofitable for you."

Hebrews 13:17

_____

_____

_____

_____

_____

E̲xamine and R̲eflect
"But let every man prove his own work, and then shall he have rejoicing in himself alone, and not in another."   Galatians 6:4

_____

_____

_____

_____

_____

_____

Notes

_____

_____

_____

_____

_____

Date_____

"Call unto Me, and I will answer thee, and shew thee great and might things, which thou knowest not. Jeremiah 33:3

Praise and Thanksgiving

"O Come, let us sing unto the LORD: let us make a joyful noise to the rock of our salvation . . . O come, let us worship and bow down: let us kneel before the LORD our Maker." Psalm 95:1, 6

_____

_____

Repent through Confession

'Therefore say thou unto them, Thus saith the LORD of hosts; Turn ye unto Me, saith the LORD of hosts, and I will turn unto you, saith the LORD of hosts." Zechariah 1:3

"Draw nigh to God, and He will draw nigh unto you. Cleanse your hands, ye sinners; and purify your hearts, ye double minded." James 4:8

_____

_____

Ask

"And all things, whatsoever ye shall ask in prayer, believing, ye shall receive. Matthew 21:22

Active Military members:

Name	Need	Date Entered	Date Answered

Missionaries

Yield to the Father (Prayer of surrender to the will of the Father)
"Nevertheless not what I will, but what thou wilt."   Mark 14:36

_____
_____
_____
_____
_____

Examine and Reflect
"Examine yourselves, whether ye be in the faith; prove your own selves.
Know ye not your own selves, how that Jesus Christ is in your, except ye
be reprobates?   2 Corinthians 13:5

_____
_____
_____
_____
_____
_____

Notes

_____
_____
_____
_____
_____
_____
_____
_____
_____
_____
_____
_____
_____
_____
_____

Date_____

"Now unto Him that is able to do exceeding abundantly above all that we ask or think, according to the power that worketh in us. Ephesians 3:20

Praise and Thanksgiving
"O Come, let us sing unto the LORD: let us make a joyful noise to the rock of our salvation . . . O come, let us worship and bow down: let us kneel before the LORD our Maker."   Psalm 95:1, 6

_____

_____

Repent through Confession
'Therefore say thou unto them, Thus saith the LORD of hosts; Turn ye unto Me, saith the LORD of hosts, and I will turn unto you, saith the LORD of hosts."   Zechariah 1:3

"Draw nigh to God, and He will draw nigh unto you. Cleanse your hands, ye sinners; and purify your hearts, ye double minded."   James 4:8

_____

_____

Ask
"As, and it shall be given you; seek, and you shall find; knock, and it shall be opened unto you: for everyone that asketh receiveth; and he that seeketh findeth; and to him that knocketh it shall be opened."
                                                        Matthew 7:7-8

Physically ill
"The prayer of faith shall save the sick, and the LORD shall raise him."
                                                          James 5:15

Name	Need	Date Entered	Date Answered

Yield to the Father (Prayer of surrender to the will of the Father)

"Know ye not, that to whom ye yield yourself servants to obey, his servants ye are to whom ye obey; whether of sin unto death, or of obedience unto righteousness?"   Romans 6:16

_____
_____
_____
_____
_____

Examine and Reflect

"Search me, O God, and know my heart: try me, and know my thoughts. And see if there be any wicked way in me, and lead me in the way everlasting."   Psalm 139:23-24

_____
_____
_____
_____
_____

Notes

_____
_____
_____
_____
_____
_____
_____
_____
_____
_____
_____
_____
_____
_____

Date_____

". . . the will of the LORD be done."   Acts 21:14

Praise and Thanksgiving
"O Come, let us sing unto the LORD: let us make a joyful noise to the rock
of our salvation . . . O come, let us worship and bow down: let us kneel
before the LORD our Maker."   Psalm 95:1, 6

_____

_____

Repent through Confession
'Therefore say thou unto them, Thus saith the LORD of hosts; Turn ye unto
Me, saith the LORD of hosts, and I will turn unto you, saith the LORD of
hosts."   Zechariah 1:3

"Draw nigh to God, and He will draw nigh unto you. Cleanse your hands,
ye sinners; and purify your hearts, ye double minded."   James 4:8

_____

_____

Ask
"But my God shall supply all your need according to His riches in glory
by Christ Jesus.   Philippians 4:19

Those with Relationship Problems:

Name	Need	Date Entered	Date Answered

<u>Y</u>ield to the Father (Prayer of surrender to the will of the Father)

"Neither yield ye your members as instruments of unrighteousness unto sin: but yield yourselves unto God, as those that are alive from the dead, and your members as instruments of righteousness unto God."

Romans 6:13

_____

_____

_____

_____

<u>E</u>xamine and <u>R</u>eflect

"Judge me, O LORD; for I have walked in my integrity; I have trusted also in the LORD; therefore I shall not slide." Psalm 26:1

_____

_____

_____

_____

_____

_____

Notes

_____

_____

_____

_____

_____

_____

_____

_____

_____

_____

_____

_____

_____

_____

Date_____

"Beloved, if our heart condemn us not, then have we confidence toward God. And whatsoever we ask, we receive of Him, because we keep His command-ments, and do those things that are pleasing in His sight.
1 John 3:21-22

Praise and Thanksgiving
"O Come, let us sing unto the LORD: let us make a joyful noise to the rock of our salvation . . . O come, let us worship and bow down: let us kneel before the LORD our Maker."
Psalm 95:1, 6

_____

_____

Repent through Confession
'Therefore say thou unto them, Thus saith the LORD of hosts; Turn ye unto Me, saith the LORD of hosts, and I will turn unto you, saith the LORD of hosts."
Zechariah 1:3

"Draw nigh to God, and He will draw nigh unto you. Cleanse your hands, ye sinners; and purify your hearts, ye double minded."
James 4:8

_____

_____

Ask
"And His disciples came to Him, and awoke Him, saying, LORD, save us: we perish. And He saith unto them, Why are ye fearful, O ye of little faith? Then He arose, and rebuked the winds and the sea; and there was great calm."
Matthew 8:26

"Likewise the Spirit also helpeth our infirmities: for we know not what we should pray for as we ought: but the Spirit itself maketh intercession for us with groanings which cannot be uttered."
Romans 8:26

Personal needs: **Date Entered**   **Date Answered**

_____

_____

Personal desires for the glory of God:

_____

_____

(Yield to the Father) Prayer of surrender to the will of the Father
"Submit yourselves therefore to God. Resist the devil, and he will flee from you."
James 4:7

_____

_____

_____

_____

_____

Examine and Reflect
"Let my cry come near before The, O LORD: give me understanding according to Thy word."
Psalm 119:169

_____

_____

_____

_____

_____

_____

Notes

_____

_____

_____

_____

_____

_____

_____

_____

_____

_____

_____

_____

Date_____

"He hears and answers every prayer, where the *true conditions* of praying are met." (*italics* inserted for emphasis)

E. M. Bounds, "The Possibilities of Prayer"

"And this is the confidence that we have in Him, that, if we ask anything according to His will, He heareth us: And if we know that He hear us, whatsoever we ask, we know that we have the petitions that we desired if Him."

I John 5:14-15

Praise and Thanksgiving

"O Come, let us sing unto the LORD: let us make a joyful noise to the rock of our salvation . . . O come, let us worship and bow down: let us kneel before the LORD our Maker."

Psalm 95:1, 6

_____

_____

Repent through Confession

'Therefore say thou unto them, Thus saith the LORD of hosts; Turn ye unto Me, saith the LORD of hosts, and I will turn unto you, saith the LORD of hosts."

Zechariah 1:3

"Draw nigh to God, and He will draw nigh unto you. Cleanse your hands, ye sinners; and purify your hearts, ye double minded."

James 4:8

_____

_____

Ask

"Ask, and it shall be given you; seek, and you shall find; knock, and it shall be opened unto you: for everyone that asketh receiveth; and he that seeketh findeth; and to him that knocketh it shall be opened."

Matthew 7:7-8

Salvation
"For by grace are you saved through faith; . . . it is the gift of God"

Ephesians 2:8

Name   **Date Entered**   **Date Answered**

_____

_____

_____

<u>Y</u>ield to the Father (Prayer of surrender to the will of the Father)
"Nevertheless not what I will, but what thou wilt."   Mark 14:36b

_____

_____

_____

_____

<u>E</u>xamine and <u>R</u>eflect
"Examine yourselves, whether ye be in faith; prove your own selves."

2 Corinthians 13:5

_____

_____

_____

_____

_____

_____

Notes

_____

_____

_____

_____

_____

_____

_____

_____

_____

Date_____

"The effectual fervent prayer of a righteous man availeth much."

James 5:16b

Praise and Thanksgiving

"O Come, let us sing unto the LORD: let us make a joyful noise to the rock of our salvation . . . O come, let us worship and bow down: let us kneel before the LORD our Maker." Psalm 95:1, 6

_____

_____

Repent through Confession

'Therefore say thou unto them, Thus saith the LORD of hosts; Turn ye unto Me, saith the LORD of hosts, and I will turn unto you, saith the LORD of hosts." Zechariah 1:3

"Draw nigh to God, and He will draw nigh unto you. Cleanse your hands, ye sinners; and purify your hearts, ye double minded." James 4:8

_____

_____

Ask

"Therefore I say unto you, What things soever ye desire, when ye pray, believe that ye receive them, and ye shall have them" Mark 11:24

Church Leadership

"Finally, brethren, pray for us, that the word of the LORD may have free course, and be glorified, as as it is with you." 2 Thessalonians 3:1

"Behold, how good and how pleasant it is for the brethren to dwell together in unity." Psalm 133:1

Senior Pastor: (Personal) _____
(Professional) _____
Associate Pastor/Administrator: (Personal) _____
(Professional) _____

Associate Pastor/Music: (Personal) _____
(Professional) _____
Associate Pastor/Education: (Personal) _____
(Professional) _____
Children's Ministry Director: (Personal) _____
(Professional) _____
Other Ministerial Staff _____
Other Ministerial Staff _____
Other Ministerial Staff _____

<u>Y</u>ield to the Father (Prayer of surrender to the will of the Father)
"Humble yourselves in the sight of the L<small>ORD</small>, and He shall lift you up.

James 4:10

_____
_____
_____
_____

<u>E</u>xamine and <u>R</u>eflect
"Examine me, O L<small>ORD</small>, and prove me: . . ."   Psalm 26:2

_____
_____
_____
_____
_____
_____
_____
_____

Date_____

"Let us therefore come boldly unto the throne of grace, that we may obtain mercy, and find grace to help in time of need.   Hebrews 4:16

Praise and Thanksgiving
"O Come, let us sing unto the LORD: let us make a joyful noise to the rock of our salvation . . . O come, let us worship and bow down: let us kneel before the LORD our Maker."   Psalm 95:1, 6

_____

_____

Repent through Confession
'Therefore say thou unto them, Thus saith the LORD of hosts; Turn ye unto Me, saith the LORD of hosts, and I will turn unto you, saith the LORD of hosts."   Zechariah 1:3

"Draw nigh to God, and He will draw nigh unto you. Cleanse your hands, ye sinners; and purify your hearts, ye double minded."   James 4:8

_____

_____

Ask
"If ye abide in Me, and my words abide in you, ye shall ask what ye will, and it shall be done unto you."   John 15:7

Government Leadership and Policy-makers
"I exhort therefore, that, first of all, supplications, prayers, intercessions, and giving of thanks be made for all men; for kings, and for all that are in authority; that we may lead a quiet and peaceable life in all godliness and honesty."   1 Timothy 2:1-3

National:_____

_____

_____

State:_____

_____

_____

Local_____

_____

_____

Yield to the Father (Prayer of surrender to the will of the Father)

"Obey them that have the rule over you, and submit yourselves: for they watch for your souls, as they that must give account, that they may do it with joy, and not with grief: for that is unprofitable for you."

Hebrews 13:17

_____

_____

_____

_____

_____

Examine and **R**eflect

"But let every man prove his own work, and then shall he have rejoicing in himself alone, and not in another." Galatians 6:4

_____

_____

_____

_____

_____

_____

Notes

_____

_____

_____

_____

_____

Date_____

"Call unto Me, and I will answer thee, and shew thee great and might things, which thou knowest not.   Jeremiah 33:3

Praise and Thanksgiving
"O Come, let us sing unto the LORD: let us make a joyful noise to the rock of our salvation . . . O come, let us worship and bow down: let us kneel before the LORD our Maker."   Psalm 95:1, 6

_____

_____

Repent through Confession
'Therefore say thou unto them, Thus saith the LORD of hosts; Turn ye unto Me, saith the LORD of hosts, and I will turn unto you, saith the LORD of hosts."   Zechariah 1:3

"Draw nigh to God, and He will draw nigh unto you. Cleanse your hands, ye sinners; and purify your hearts, ye double minded."   James 4:8

_____

_____

Ask
"And all things, whatsoever ye shall ask in prayer, believing, ye shall receive.   Matthew 21:22

Active Military members:

Name	Need	Date Entered	Date Answered

Missionaries

_____

_____

_____

_____

Yield to the Father (Prayer of surrender to the will of the Father)
"Nevertheless not what I will, but what thou wilt."   Mark 14:36

_____

_____

_____

_____

_____

Examine and Reflect
"Examine yourselves, whether ye be in the faith; prove your own selves.
Know ye not your own selves, how that Jesus Christ is in your, except ye
be reprobates?   2 Corinthians 13:5

_____

_____

_____

_____

_____

_____

Notes

_____

_____

_____

_____

_____

_____

_____

_____

_____

_____

_____

_____

_____

_____

_____

Date_____

"Now unto Him that is able to do exceeding abundantly above all that we ask or think, according to the power that worketh in us. Ephesians 3:20

Praise and Thanksgiving
"O Come, let us sing unto the LORD: let us make a joyful noise to the rock of our salvation . . . O come, let us worship and bow down: let us kneel before the LORD our Maker."   Psalm 95:1, 6

_____

_____

Repent through Confession
'Therefore say thou unto them, Thus saith the LORD of hosts; Turn ye unto Me, saith the LORD of hosts, and I will turn unto you, saith the LORD of hosts."   Zechariah 1:3

"Draw nigh to God, and He will draw nigh unto you. Cleanse your hands, ye sinners; and purify your hearts, ye double minded."   James 4:8

_____

_____

Ask
"As, and it shall be given you; seek, and you shall find; knock, and it shall be opened unto you: for everyone that asketh receiveth; and he that seeketh findeth; and to him that knocketh it shall be opened."
                                                           Matthew 7:7-8

Physically ill
"The prayer of faith shall save the sick, and the LORD shall raise him."
                                                           James 5:15

Name	Need	Date Entered	Date Answered

Yield to the Father (Prayer of surrender to the will of the Father)

"Know ye not, that to whom ye yield yourself servants to obey, his servants ye are to whom ye obey; whether of sin unto death, or of obedience unto righteousness?"   Romans 6:16

_____

_____

_____

_____

_____

Examine and Reflect

"Search me, O God, and know my heart: try me, and know my thoughts. And see if there be any wicked way in me, and lead me in the way everlasting."   Psalm 139:23-24

_____

_____

_____

_____

_____

_____

Notes

_____

_____

_____

_____

_____

_____

_____

_____

_____

_____

_____

_____

_____

Date_____

". . . the will of the LORD be done."   Acts 21:14

Praise and Thanksgiving
"O Come, let us sing unto the LORD: let us make a joyful noise to the rock
of our salvation . . . O come, let us worship and bow down: let us kneel
before the LORD our Maker."   Psalm 95:1, 6

_____

_____

Repent through Confession
'Therefore say thou unto them, Thus saith the LORD of hosts; Turn ye unto
Me, saith the LORD of hosts, and I will turn unto you, saith the LORD of
hosts."   Zechariah 1:3

"Draw nigh to God, and He will draw nigh unto you. Cleanse your hands,
ye sinners; and purify your hearts, ye double minded."   James 4:8

_____

_____

Ask
"But my God shall supply all your need according to His riches in glory
by Christ Jesus.   Philippians 4:19

Those with Relationship Problems:

Name	Need	Date Entered	Date Answered

<u>Y</u>ield to the Father (Prayer of surrender to the will of the Father)

"Neither yield ye your members as instruments of unrighteousness unto sin: but yield yourselves unto God, as those that are alive from the dead, and your members as instruments of righteousness unto God."

Romans 6:13

_____

_____

_____

_____

<u>E</u>xamine and <u>R</u>eflect

"Judge me, O Lord; for I have walked in my integrity; I have trusted also in the Lord; therefore I shall not slide."

Psalm 26:1

_____

_____

_____

_____

_____

_____

Notes

_____

_____

_____

_____

_____

_____

_____

_____

_____

_____

_____

_____

Date_____

"Beloved, if our heart condemn us not, then have we confidence toward God. And whatsoever we ask, we receive of Him, because we keep His command-ments, and do those things that are pleasing in His sight.   1 John 3:21-22

Praise and Thanksgiving
"O Come, let us sing unto the LORD: let us make a joyful noise to the rock of our salvation . . . O come, let us worship and bow down: let us kneel before the LORD our Maker."   Psalm 95:1, 6

_____

_____

Repent through Confession
'Therefore say thou unto them, Thus saith the LORD of hosts; Turn ye unto Me, saith the LORD of hosts, and I will turn unto you, saith the LORD of hosts."   Zechariah 1:3

"Draw nigh to God, and He will draw nigh unto you. Cleanse your hands, ye sinners; and purify your hearts, ye double minded."   James 4:8

_____

_____

Ask
"And His disciples came to Him, and awoke Him, saying, LORD, save us: we perish. And He saith unto them, Why are ye fearful, O ye of little faith? Then He arose, and rebuked the winds and the sea; and there was great calm."   Matthew 8:26

"Likewise the Spirit also helpeth our infirmities: for we know not what we should pray for as we ought: but the Spirit itself maketh intercession for us with groanings which cannot be uttered."   Romans 8:26

Personal needs: **Date Entered**   **Date Answered**

_____

_____

Personal desires for the glory of God:

_____

_____

(Yield to the Father) Prayer of surrender to the will of the Father

"Submit yourselves therefore to God. Resist the devil, and he will flee from you."

James 4:7

_____

_____

_____

_____

_____

Examine and Reflect

"Let my cry come near before The, O LORD: give me understanding according to Thy word."`

Psalm 119:169

_____

_____

_____

_____

_____

_____

Notes

_____

_____

_____

_____

_____

_____

_____

_____

_____

_____

Date_____

"He hears and answers every prayer, where the *true conditions* of praying are met." (*italics* inserted for emphasis)

E. M. Bounds, "The Possibilities of Prayer"

"And this is the confidence that we have in Him, that, if we ask anything according to His will, He heareth us: And if we know that He hear us, whatsoever we ask, we know that we have the petitions that we desired if Him."

I John 5:14-15

Praise and Thanksgiving
"O Come, let us sing unto the LORD: let us make a joyful noise to the rock of our salvation . . . O come, let us worship and bow down: let us kneel before the LORD our Maker."

Psalm 95:1, 6

_____

_____

Repent through Confession
'Therefore say thou unto them, Thus saith the LORD of hosts; Turn ye unto Me, saith the LORD of hosts, and I will turn unto you, saith the LORD of hosts."

Zechariah 1:3

"Draw nigh to God, and He will draw nigh unto you. Cleanse your hands, ye sinners; and purify your hearts, ye double minded."

James 4:8

_____

_____

Ask
"Ask, and it shall be given you; seek, and you shall find; knock, and it shall be opened unto you: for everyone that asketh receiveth; and he that seeketh findeth; and to him that knocketh it shall be opened."

Matthew 7:7-8

Salvation

"For by grace are you saved through faith; . . . it is the gift of God"

Ephesians 2:8

Name   **Date Entered**   **Date Answered**

_____

_____

_____

Yield to the Father (Prayer of surrender to the will of the Father)

"Nevertheless not what I will, but what thou wilt."   Mark 14:36b

_____

_____

_____

_____

Examine and Reflect

"Examine yourselves, whether ye be in faith; prove your own selves."

2 Corinthians 13:5

_____

_____

_____

_____

_____

_____

Notes

_____

_____

_____

_____

_____

_____

_____

_____

Date_____

"The effectual fervent prayer of a righteous man availeth much."

James 5:16b

Praise and Thanksgiving

"O Come, let us sing unto the LORD: let us make a joyful noise to the rock of our salvation . . . O come, let us worship and bow down: let us kneel before the LORD our Maker."

Psalm 95:1, 6

_____

_____

Repent through Confession

'Therefore say thou unto them, Thus saith the LORD of hosts; Turn ye unto Me, saith the LORD of hosts, and I will turn unto you, saith the LORD of hosts."

Zechariah 1:3

"Draw nigh to God, and He will draw nigh unto you. Cleanse your hands, ye sinners; and purify your hearts, ye double minded."

James 4:8

_____

_____

Ask

"Therefore I say unto you, What things soever ye desire, when ye pray, believe that ye receive them, and ye shall have them"

Mark 11:24

Church Leadership

"Finally, brethren, pray for us, that the word of the LORD may have free course, and be glorified, as as it is with you."

2 Thessalonians 3:1

"Behold, how good and how pleasant it is for the brethren to dwell together in unity."

Psalm 133:1

Senior Pastor: (Personal) _____

(Professional) _____

Associate Pastor/Administrator: (Personal) _____

(Professional) _____

Associate Pastor/Music: (Personal) _____
(Professional) _____
Associate Pastor/Education: (Personal) _____
(Professional) _____
Children's Ministry Director: (Personal) _____
(Professional) _____
Other Ministerial Staff _____
Other Ministerial Staff _____
Other Ministerial Staff _____

Yield to the Father (Prayer of surrender to the will of the Father)

"Humble yourselves in the sight of the LORD, and He shall lift you up.

James 4:10

_____
_____
_____
_____

Examine and Reflect

"Examine me, O LORD, and prove me: . . ."   Psalm 26:2

_____
_____
_____
_____
_____
_____
_____

Date_____

"Let us therefore come boldly unto the throne of grace, that we may obtain mercy, and find grace to help in time of need.   Hebrews 4:16

Praise and Thanksgiving
"O Come, let us sing unto the LORD: let us make a joyful noise to the rock of our salvation . . . O come, let us worship and bow down: let us kneel before the LORD our Maker."   Psalm 95:1, 6

_____

_____

Repent through Confession
'Therefore say thou unto them, Thus saith the LORD of hosts; Turn ye unto Me, saith the LORD of hosts, and I will turn unto you, saith the LORD of hosts."   Zechariah 1:3

"Draw nigh to God, and He will draw nigh unto you. Cleanse your hands, ye sinners; and purify your hearts, ye double minded."   James 4:8

_____

_____

Ask
"If ye abide in Me, and my words abide in you, ye shall ask what ye will, and it shall be done unto you."   John 15:7

Government Leadership and Policy-makers
"I exhort therefore, that, first of all, supplications, prayers, intercessions, and giving of thanks be made for all men; for kings, and for all that are in authority; that we may lead a quiet and peaceable life in all godliness and honesty."   1 Timothy 2:1-3

National:_____

_____

_____

State:_____

_____

_____

Local_____

_____

_____

Yield to the Father (Prayer of surrender to the will of the Father)
"Obey them that have the rule over you, and submit yourselves: for they watch for your souls, as they that must give account, that they may do it with joy, and not with grief: for that is unprofitable for you."

Hebrews 13:17

_____

_____

_____

_____

_____

Examine and **R**eflect
"But let every man prove his own work, and then shall he have rejoicing in himself alone, and not in another." Galatians 6:4

_____

_____

_____

_____

_____

_____

Notes

_____

_____

_____

_____

_____

Date_____

"Call unto Me, and I will answer thee, and shew thee great and might things, which thou knowest not.   Jeremiah 33:3

Praise and Thanksgiving

"I will praise Thee with my whole heart: before the gods will I sing praise unto Thee. I will worship toward Thy holy temple, and praise Thy name for Thy lovingkindness and for Thy truth: for Thou hast magnified Thy word above all Thy name.   Psalm 138: 1-2

Repentance through Confession

"Create in me a clean heart, O, God; and renew a right spirit within me . . . . Restore unto me the joy of Thy salvation.   Psalm 51:10, 12

Ask

"And all things, whatsoever ye shall ask in prayer, believing, ye shall receive.   Matthew 21:22

Active Military members:

Name	Need	Date Entered	Date Answered

Missionaries

Yield to the Father (Prayer of surrender to the will of the Father)

"Nevertheless not what I will, but what thou wilt."   Mark 14:36

Examine and **R**eflect

"Examine yourselves, whether ye be in the faith; prove your own selves. Know ye not your own selves, how that Jesus Christ is in your, except ye be reprobates?

2 Corinthians 13:5

_____

_____

_____

_____

_____

_____

Notes

_____

_____

_____

_____

_____

_____

_____

_____

_____

_____

_____

_____

_____

_____

_____

_____

_____

_____

_____

_____

_____

Date_____

"Now unto Him that is able to do exceeding abundantly above all that we ask or think, according to the power that worketh in us. Ephesians 3:20

Praise and Thanksgiving
"O Come, let us sing unto the LORD: let us make a joyful noise to the rock of our salvation . . . O come, let us worship and bow down: let us kneel before the LORD our Maker."   Psalm 95:1, 6

_____

_____

Repent through Confession
'Therefore say thou unto them, Thus saith the LORD of hosts; Turn ye unto Me, saith the LORD of hosts, and I will turn unto you, saith the LORD of hosts."   Zechariah 1:3

"Draw nigh to God, and He will draw nigh unto you. Cleanse your hands, ye sinners; and purify your hearts, ye double minded."   James 4:8

_____

_____

Ask
"As, and it shall be given you; seek, and you shall find; knock, and it shall be opened unto you: for everyone that asketh receiveth; and he that seeketh findeth; and to him that knocketh it shall be opened."
                                                          Matthew 7:7-8

Physically ill
"The prayer of faith shall save the sick, and the LORD shall raise him."
                                                            James 5:15

Name	Need	Date Entered	Date Answered

Yield to the Father (Prayer of surrender to the will of the Father)

"Know ye not, that to whom ye yield yourself servants to obey, his servants ye are to whom ye obey; whether of sin unto death, or of obedience unto righteousness?"

Romans 6:16

_____

_____

_____

_____

_____

Examine and Reflect

"Search me, O God, and know my heart: try me, and know my thoughts. And see if there be any wicked way in me, and lead me in the way everlasting."

Psalm 139:23-24

_____

_____

_____

_____

_____

_____

Notes

_____

_____

_____

_____

_____

_____

_____

_____

_____

_____

_____

_____

_____

Date_____

"... the will of the LORD be done." Acts 21:14

Praise and Thanksgiving
"O Come, let us sing unto the LORD: let us make a joyful noise to the rock of our salvation ... O come, let us worship and bow down: let us kneel before the LORD our Maker." Psalm 95:1, 6

_____

_____

Repent through Confession
'Therefore say thou unto them, Thus saith the LORD of hosts; Turn ye unto Me, saith the LORD of hosts, and I will turn unto you, saith the LORD of hosts." Zechariah 1:3

"Draw nigh to God, and He will draw nigh unto you. Cleanse your hands, ye sinners; and purify your hearts, ye double minded." James 4:8

_____

_____

Ask
"But my God shall supply all your need according to His riches in glory by Christ Jesus. Philippians 4:19

Those with Relationship Problems:

Name	Need	Date Entered	Date Answered

Yield to the Father (Prayer of surrender to the will of the Father)
"Neither yield ye your members as instruments of unrighteousness unto
sin: but yield yourselves unto God, as those that are alive from the dead,
and your members as instruments of righteousness unto God."

Romans 6:13

_____

_____

_____

_____

Examine and Reflect
"Judge me, O LORD; for I have walked in my integrity; I have trusted also
in the LORD; therefore I shall not slide."

Psalm 26:1

_____

_____

_____

_____

_____

_____

Notes

_____

_____

_____

_____

_____

_____

_____

_____

_____

_____

_____

_____

Date_____

"Beloved, if our heart condemn us not, then have we confidence toward God. And whatsoever we ask, we receive of Him, because we keep His command-ments, and do those things that are pleasing in His sight.
1 John 3:21-22

Praise and Thanksgiving
"O Come, let us sing unto the LORD: let us make a joyful noise to the rock of our salvation . . . O come, let us worship and bow down: let us kneel before the LORD our Maker."
Psalm 95:1, 6

_____

_____

Repent through Confession
'Therefore say thou unto them, Thus saith the LORD of hosts; Turn ye unto Me, saith the LORD of hosts, and I will turn unto you, saith the LORD of hosts."
Zechariah 1:3

"Draw nigh to God, and He will draw nigh unto you. Cleanse your hands, ye sinners; and purify your hearts, ye double minded."
James 4:8

_____

_____

Ask
"And His disciples came to Him, and awoke Him, saying, LORD, save us: we perish. And He saith unto them, Why are ye fearful, O ye of little faith? Then He arose, and rebuked the winds and the sea; and there was great calm."
Matthew 8:26

"Likewise the Spirit also helpeth our infirmities: for we know not what we should pray for as we ought: but the Spirit itself maketh intercession for us with groanings which cannot be uttered."
Romans 8:26

Personal needs: **Date Entered**   **Date Answered**

_____

_____

Personal desires for the glory of God:

_____

_____

(Y̲ield to the Father) Prayer of surrender to the will of the Father
"Submit yourselves therefore to God. Resist the devil, and he will flee from you."

James 4:7

_____

_____

_____

_____

_____

E̲xamine and R̲eflect
"Let my cry come near before The, O LORD: give me understanding according to Thy word."

Psalm 119:169

_____

_____

_____

_____

_____

_____

Notes

_____

_____

_____

_____

_____

_____

_____

_____

_____

Date_____

"He hears and answers every prayer, where the *true conditions* of praying are met." (*italics* inserted for emphasis)

E. M. Bounds, "The Possibilities of Prayer"

"And this is the confidence that we have in Him, that, if we ask anything according to His will, He heareth us: And if we know that He hear us, whatsoever we ask, we know that we have the petitions that we desired if Him."

I John 5:14-15

Praise and Thanksgiving

"O Come, let us sing unto the LORD: let us make a joyful noise to the rock of our salvation . . . O come, let us worship and bow down: let us kneel before the LORD our Maker."

Psalm 95:1, 6

_____

_____

Repent through Confession

'Therefore say thou unto them, Thus saith the LORD of hosts; Turn ye unto Me, saith the LORD of hosts, and I will turn unto you, saith the LORD of hosts."

Zechariah 1:3

"Draw nigh to God, and He will draw nigh unto you. Cleanse your hands, ye sinners; and purify your hearts, ye double minded."

James 4:8

_____

_____

Ask

"Ask, and it shall be given you; seek, and you shall find; knock, and it shall be opened unto you: for everyone that asketh receiveth; and he that seeketh findeth; and to him that knocketh it shall be opened."

Matthew 7:7-8

Salvation

"For by grace are you saved through faith; . . . it is the gift of God"

Ephesians 2:8

Name	Date Entered	Date Answered

Yield to the Father (Prayer of surrender to the will of the Father)

"Nevertheless not what I will, but what thou wilt."   Mark 14:36b

Examine and Reflect

"Examine yourselves, whether ye be in faith; prove your own selves."

2 Corinthians 13:5

Notes

Date_____

"The effectual fervent prayer of a righteous man availeth much."

James 5:16b

Praise and Thanksgiving
"O Come, let us sing unto the LORD: let us make a joyful noise to the rock of our salvation . . . O come, let us worship and bow down: let us kneel before the LORD our Maker." Psalm 95:1, 6

_____

_____

Repent through Confession
'Therefore say thou unto them, Thus saith the LORD of hosts; Turn ye unto Me, saith the LORD of hosts, and I will turn unto you, saith the LORD of hosts." Zechariah 1:3

"Draw nigh to God, and He will draw nigh unto you. Cleanse your hands, ye sinners; and purify your hearts, ye double minded." James 4:8

_____

_____

Ask
"Therefore I say unto you, What things soever ye desire, when ye pray, believe that ye receive them, and ye shall have them" Mark 11:24

Church Leadership
"Finally, brethren, pray for us, that the word of the LORD may have free course, and be glorified, as as it is with you." 2 Thessalonians 3:1

"Behold, how good and how pleasant it is for the brethren to dwell together in unity." Psalm 133:1

Senior Pastor: (Personal) _____

(Professional) _____

Associate Pastor/Administrator: (Personal) _____

(Professional) _____

Associate Pastor/Music: (Personal) _____
(Professional) _____
Associate Pastor/Education: (Personal) _____
(Professional) _____
Children's Ministry Director: (Personal) _____
(Professional) _____
Other Ministerial Staff _____
Other Ministerial Staff _____
Other Ministerial Staff _____

Yield to the Father (Prayer of surrender to the will of the Father)
"Humble yourselves in the sight of the LORD, and He shall lift you up.
James 4:10

_____
_____
_____
_____

Examine and **R**eflect
"Examine me, O LORD, and prove me: . . ."   Psalm 26:2

_____
_____
_____
_____
_____
_____
_____
_____

Date_____

"Let us therefore come boldly unto the throne of grace, that we may obtain mercy, and find grace to help in time of need.　　Hebrews 4:16

Praise and Thanksgiving

"I will lift up mine eyes unto the hills from whence cometh my help. My help cometh from the LORD, which made heaven and earth.
　　　　　　　　　　　　　　　　　　Psalm 121:1-2

Repentance through Confession

"For I acknowledge my transgressions: and my sin is ever before me. Against Thee, and Thee only, have I sinned, and done this evil in Thy sight: that Thou mightest be justified when Thou speakest, and be clear when Thou judgest.　　　　　　　　　Psalm 51:3-4

Ask

"If ye abide in Me, and my words abide in you, ye shall ask what ye will, and it shall be done unto you."　　　　　　　　　John 15:7

Government Leadership and Policy-makers

"I exhort therefore, that, first of all, supplications, prayers, intercessions, and giving of thanks be made for all men; for kings, and for all that are in authority; that we may lead a quiet and peaceable life in all godliness and honesty."　　　　　　　　　　　　　　1 Timothy 2:1-3

_____
_____
_____
_____
_____
_____
_____
_____
_____
_____
_____
_____

Yield to the Father (Prayer of surrender to the will of the Father)
"Obey them that have the rule over you, and submit yourselves: for they watch for your souls, as they that must give account, that they may do it with joy, and not with grief: for that is unprofitable for you."

Hebrews 13:17

_____

_____

_____

_____

_____

Examine and **R**eflect
"But let every man prove his own work, and then shall he have rejoicing in himself alone, and not in another."

Galatians 6:4

_____

_____

_____

_____

_____

_____

Notes

_____

_____

_____

_____

_____

_____

_____

_____

_____

_____

_____

_____

_____

Date_____

"Call unto Me, and I will answer thee, and shew thee great and might things, which thou knowest not.   Jeremiah 33:3

Praise and Thanksgiving

"O Come, let us sing unto the LORD: let us make a joyful noise to the rock of our salvation . . . O come, let us worship and bow down: let us kneel before the LORD our Maker."   Psalm 95:1, 6

_____

_____

Repent through Confession

'Therefore say thou unto them, Thus saith the LORD of hosts; Turn ye unto Me, saith the LORD of hosts, and I will turn unto you, saith the LORD of hosts."   Zechariah 1:3

"Draw nigh to God, and He will draw nigh unto you. Cleanse your hands, ye sinners; and purify your hearts, ye double minded."   James 4:8

_____

_____

Ask

"And all things, whatsoever ye shall ask in prayer, believing, ye shall receive.   Matthew 21:22

Active Military members:

Name	Need	Date Entered	Date Answered

Missionaries

_____

_____

_____

_____

<u>Y</u>ield to the Father (Prayer of surrender to the will of the Father)

"Nevertheless not what I will, but what thou wilt."   Mark 14:36

_____

_____

_____

_____

_____

<u>E</u>xamine and <u>R</u>eflect

"Examine yourselves, whether ye be in the faith; prove your own selves. Know ye not your own selves, how that Jesus Christ is in your, except ye be reprobates?   2 Corinthians 13:5

_____

_____

_____

_____

_____

Notes

_____

_____

_____

_____

_____

_____

_____

_____

_____

_____

_____

_____

_____

_____

Date_____

"Now unto Him that is able to do exceeding abundantly above all that we ask or think, according to the power that worketh in us. Ephesians 3:20

Praise and Thanksgiving
"O Come, let us sing unto the LORD: let us make a joyful noise to the rock of our salvation . . . O come, let us worship and bow down: let us kneel before the LORD our Maker."   Psalm 95:1, 6

_____

_____

Repent through Confession
'Therefore say thou unto them, Thus saith the LORD of hosts; Turn ye unto Me, saith the LORD of hosts, and I will turn unto you, saith the LORD of hosts."   Zechariah 1:3

"Draw nigh to God, and He will draw nigh unto you. Cleanse your hands, ye sinners; and purify your hearts, ye double minded."   James 4:8

_____

_____

Ask
"As, and it shall be given you; seek, and you shall find; knock, and it shall be opened unto you: for everyone that asketh receiveth; and he that seeketh findeth; and to him that knocketh it shall be opened."
                                                        Matthew 7:7-8

Physically ill
"The prayer of faith shall save the sick, and the LORD shall raise him."
                                                        James 5:15

Name	Need	Date Entered	Date Answered

Yield to the Father (Prayer of surrender to the will of the Father)

"Know ye not, that to whom ye yield yourself servants to obey, his servants ye are to whom ye obey; whether of sin unto death, or of obedience unto righteousness?"   Romans 6:16

_____

_____

_____

_____

_____

Examine and Reflect

"Search me, O God, and know my heart: try me, and know my thoughts. And see if there be any wicked way in me, and lead me in the way everlasting."   Psalm 139:23-24

_____

_____

_____

_____

_____

_____

Notes

_____

_____

_____

_____

_____

_____

_____

_____

_____

_____

_____

_____

_____

Date_____

". . . the will of the LORD be done."   Acts 21:14

Praise and Thanksgiving
"O Come, let us sing unto the LORD: let us make a joyful noise to the rock of our salvation . . . O come, let us worship and bow down: let us kneel before the LORD our Maker."   Psalm 95:1, 6

_____

_____

Repent through Confession
'Therefore say thou unto them, Thus saith the LORD of hosts; Turn ye unto Me, saith the LORD of hosts, and I will turn unto you, saith the LORD of hosts."   Zechariah 1:3

"Draw nigh to God, and He will draw nigh unto you. Cleanse your hands, ye sinners; and purify your hearts, ye double minded."   James 4:8

_____

_____

Ask
"But my God shall supply all your need according to His riches in glory by Christ Jesus.   Philippians 4:19

Those with Relationship Problems:
Name	Need	Date Entered	Date Answered

Yield to the Father (Prayer of surrender to the will of the Father)

"Neither yield ye your members as instruments of unrighteousness unto sin: but yield yourselves unto God, as those that are alive from the dead, and your members as instruments of righteousness unto God."

Romans 6:13

_____

_____

_____

_____

Examine and Reflect

"Judge me, O Lord; for I have walked in my integrity; I have trusted also in the Lord; therefore I shall not slide." Psalm 26:1

_____

_____

_____

_____

_____

_____

Notes

_____

_____

_____

_____

_____

_____

_____

_____

_____

_____

_____

_____

Date_____

"Beloved, if our heart condemn us not, then have we confidence toward God. And whatsoever we ask, we receive of Him, because we keep His commandments, and do those things that are pleasing in His sight.

1 John 3:21-22

Praise and Thanksgiving
"O Come, let us sing unto the LORD: let us make a joyful noise to the rock of our salvation . . . O come, let us worship and bow down: let us kneel before the LORD our Maker."   Psalm 95:1, 6

_____

_____

Repent through Confession
'Therefore say thou unto them, Thus saith the LORD of hosts; Turn ye unto Me, saith the LORD of hosts, and I will turn unto you, saith the LORD of hosts."   Zechariah 1:3

"Draw nigh to God, and He will draw nigh unto you. Cleanse your hands, ye sinners; and purify your hearts, ye double minded."   James 4:8

_____

_____

Ask
"And His disciples came to Him, and awoke Him, saying, LORD, save us: we perish. And He saith unto them, Why are ye fearful, O ye of little faith? Then He arose, and rebuked the winds and the sea; and there was great calm."   Matthew 8:26

"Likewise the Spirit also helpeth our infirmities: for we know not what we should pray for as we ought: but the Spirit itself maketh intercession for us with groanings which cannot be uttered."   Romans 8:26

Personal needs: **Date Entered**   **Date Answered**

_____

_____

Personal desires for the glory of God:

_____

_____

(<u>Y</u>ield to the Father) Prayer of surrender to the will of the Father
"Submit yourselves therefore to God. Resist the devil, and he will flee
from you."   James 4:7

_____

_____

_____

_____

_____

<u>E</u>xamine and <u>R</u>eflect
"Let my cry come near before The, O LORD: give me understanding
according to Thy word."   Psalm 119:169

_____

_____

_____

_____

_____

_____

Notes

_____

_____

_____

_____

_____

_____

_____

_____

_____

_____

ABOUT THE
AUTHOR

D r. Ralph Spiller is an avid student of the Bible, as well as a pastor, a teacher, and a Christian counselor. He has had the privilege of sharing the Word of God with many people to the glory of God through each of these vocations for the past thirty-five years. During these opportunities to share the Word of God, prayer has been a significant part of his communion with God. In a recent search for a prayer journal with a format such as presented here, he could find none.

After retiring from the US Navy following twenty-one years of service, his career specialty made a dramatic change. He entered the ministry, serving as a prison chaplain and bi-vocational pastor to churches in southeastern Alabama and northwestern and central Florida. His prison chaplaincy experience further led to his becoming involved with Christian counseling. The spiritual need is the greatest need of man and woman, for as Jesus has said, "For what shall it profit a man, if he shall gain the whole world and lose his own soul?" (Mark 8:36).

Dr. Spiller has lived in Marion County, Florida, with his wife, Barbara, since 1985. There he served the Florida Correctional Institution as chaplain and churches as a pastor. He has also worked with mental health agencies and private practice, where he counseled many individuals, families and children.

Ralph and Barbara have two adult daughters who have blessed them with six grandchildren and one great-grandson. They enjoy traveling and being with their family.